ANNOUNCING THE HAVERGAL EDITION
NOW IN PREPARATION FOR PUBLICATION

The edition of *The Complete Works of Frances Ridley Havergal* has five parts:

Volume I *Behold Your King:*
      The Complete Poetical Works of Frances Ridley Havergal

Volume II *Whose I Am and Whom I Serve:*
      Prose Works of Frances Ridley Havergal

Volume III *Loving Messages for the Little Ones:*
      Works for Children by Frances Ridley Havergal

Volume IV *Love for Love: Frances Ridley Havergal:*
      Memorials, Letters and Biographical Works

Volume V *Songs of Truth and Love:*
      Music by Frances Ridley Havergal and William Henry Havergal

David L. Chalkley, Editor   Dr. Glen T. Wegge, Music Editor

The Music of Frances Ridley Havergal by Glen T. Wegge, Ph.D.

This Companion Volume to the Havergal edition is a valuable presentation of F.R.H.'s extant scores. Except for a very few of her hymn scores published in hymnbooks, most or nearly all of F.R.H.'s scores have been very little—if any at all—seen, or even known of, for nearly a century. What a valuable body of music has been unknown for so long and is now made available to many. Dr. Wegge completed his Ph.D. in Music Theory at Indiana University at Bloomington, and his diligence and thoroughness in this volume are obvious. First an analysis of F.R.H.'s compositions is given, an essay that both addresses the most advanced musicians and also reaches those who are untrained in music; then all the extant scores that have been found are newly typeset, with complete texts for each score and extensive indices at the end of the book. This volume presents F.R.H.'s music in newly typeset scores diligently prepared by Dr. Wegge, and Volume V of the Havergal edition presents the scores in facsimile, the original 19th century scores. (The essay—a dissertation—analysing her scores is given the same both in this Companion Volume and in Volume V of the Havergal edition.)

Dr. Wegge is also preparing all of these scores for publication in performance folio editions.

An undated photograph of Frances Ridley Havergal.

CLEAR FLOWER VASES

FOR

THE KING'S MINSTRELS.

BY

FRANCES RIDLEY HAVERGAL.

" 'Tis the essence of existence,
Rarely rising to the light:
And the songs that echo longest,
Deepest, fullest, truest, strongest,
With your life-blood you will write."
—F. R. H.

"Knowing her intense desire that Christ should be magnified, whether
by her life or in her death, may it be to His glory
that in these pages she, being dead,
'Yet speaketh !' "

Taken from the Edition of *The Complete Works of Frances Ridley Havergal.*

David L. Chalkley, Editor   Dr. Glen T. Wegge, Associate Editor

ISBN 978-1-937236-20-5   Library of Congress: 2011919009

Book cover by Sherry Goodwin and David Carter.

Prefatory Note.

THE following Papers on Modern Hymns and Hymn-Writers were contributed by the Author to "*The Day of Days.*"

Emphatically one of God's own poets, Frances Ridley Havergal could well appreciate the consecrated gift in others. Her selection of some of the Modern Hymns that are already in the Church of Christ "as household words," will commend itself to all; but an additional interest will be felt in the connecting comments—"the poetry of prose"—in which much of her own life-story and spiritual experience during the later years of her life will be read especially by those who knew her best. The Great Tunist had indeed laid His hand of love upon her; and as she wrote and sang, others heard more and more perfectly the melody of the growing life of service and praise— praise which almost antedated her entrance within the Palace Gates.

THE EDITOR OF
"THE DAY OF DAYS."

BLACKHEATH, S.E.,
November, 1881.

[Note: This book was first named *Specimen Glasses for the King's Minstrels*, and because the meaning of the phrase has so greatly changed, with now a completey different—and for this purpose undesirable—meaning, the name has been changed now to *Clear Small Vasses for the King's Minstrels*. Early in the 21st century, the phrase "specimen glass" has a very different meaning and less-than-pleasant association for medical tests in a physician's office or a hospital. In the 19th century, the phrase "specimen glass" had a completely different—and very beautiful— meaning: a slender glass vase (or other displaying container) to hold and present a flower or flowers. This is clearly, unmistakeably what was meant here, and Frances' first sentence on the next page says this beautifully. Written as magazine articles, these were gathered and published as this book posthumously. Frances had not finished a "Specimen Glass" on the hymns of Horatius Bonar when she died (see page 80 and pages 83–95 of this book). The Editor of *The Day of Days* magazine was Frances' friend, senior colleague, and publisher, Rev. Charles Bullock. David Chalkley]

INTRODUCTORY.

"SPECIMEN-GLASSES" are small, clear, and colourless vases, not intended to attract admiration or attention, but only to serve the purpose of presenting choice single specimens of roses or other flowers, whose special beauty might be overlooked in a larger vase or a crowded cluster. In the same way these little papers are not intended to be elaborate and noticeable essays on modern Hymns or Hymn-writers, but only to be the means of presenting some beautiful hymns to the reader which might otherwise escape notice in the larger collections in which they occur.

It is a very old story to talk about "flowers of poesie." But the oldest ideas are not always the worst, and the expression perhaps is most applicable to all true and worthy *Hymns.* Far-wafted fragrance, exquisite workmanship, delicate and striking beauty of form and colour, stores of hidden honey, are not the only points of comparison. There should be in every such flower incorruptible seed, which may spring up in the heart of many a gatherer; blossoming there in the beauty of holiness, and bearing fruit unto life eternal. Although many a Hymn may, flower-like, fade and pass away from remembrance, having fulfilled some lowly mission of solace to a few, or, it may be, only to one, other Hymns are true amaranths, and never die, rather gaining than losing the power of their fragrance and loveliness as years and even centuries pass on. On those which have thus become treasures of the Church, and the Home, we shall not touch; but we propose to gather a few for our Specimen-Glasses which are comparatively less known, and recently produced.

[This introduction seems to be written by F.R.H. The writing appears to be— is very much like—her writing. Published posthumously, she would likely have named this either "Preface" or "Introduction."]

This is the first page of a manuscript score composed by F.R.H. Specimen Glasses for the King's Minstrels *was a collection of magazine articles by Frances on various hymnwriters, ending with* Chapter XI, "Mission Hymns." *After that are added the last "Specimen Glass" by F.R.H., an unfinished one on hymns by Horatius Bonar; then a "Specimen Glass" by F.R.H.'s oldest sister, Miriam Crane, on Frances' hymns; and finally one by Miriam on hymns by their father, William Henry Havergal. Frances was a rarely, very finely gifted musician and composer, and she composed music for several of her own hymns as well as music for hymns by others. See Volume V of the Havergal edition,* Songs of Truth and Love: Music by Frances Ridley Havergal and William Henry Havergal.

CONTENTS.

ADDENDA.

From a Photograph by B. W. BENTLEY, *Manchester.*

William Pennefather (1816–1873).

I.

THE REV. W. PENNEFATHER'S HYMNS.

IT seems that God sends among us living illustrations of what He would have us learn, and that the lives of some of His people are like valuable engravings set between the other leaves of His great lesson-books. Engravings! yes, the word is suggestive; for it is not without sharp graving-tools and great cost and special skill and labour that these living pictures are prepared for their position. Perhaps no more perfect "proof" has ever been given for our study than one beneath which the inscription reads unmistakably thus—"The Power of Holiness." The "*beauty* of holiness" has often been shown and recognised, but perhaps we needed a grand illustration of its power. It has been given, and the portrait bears the name of William Pennefather.

Where the holiness really is, there is always the proportioned power, felt even if resisted, and none the less strong because it is secret. Why was he able to do so much more than others? so much more than men of greater physical and intellectual strength? No one spoke of him as a talented man, but as a holy man, wholly consecrated to his holy Master.

"Dedicated! He was indeed dedicated, his substance was dedicated, his time was dedicated, his poor, frail body was dedicated, even to the very last, to his Father; his natural amiability was dedicated; he lived only for one thing."

This seems to be the key to the almost unparalleled influence of his life. It was at once intense and far-reaching.

Those who came in personal contact bear witness to it, not by empty words, but by lives changed, brightened, elevated, stimulated, stirred, up, sanctified. A noble band of workers sprang up around him, working themselves and setting others, far and near, to work also. Merely to read over a bare list of what he actually *did*, almost takes away one's breath. One marvels how any one life could produce such results; and yet that life was cut off long before the years were full. The churches, the schools, the institutions, the conferences, the missions, the homes,—hardly a possible device for practical, spiritual, or temporal benefits, to all classes, but he had set it on foot. And so marvellous was his organization of all, so far-seeing was his training and placing of workers, that nothing needed to halt or suffer when the hand that set all in motion was withdrawn.

It was not North London alone that felt his power. Were there *any* of the thousands who came each June from all parts of the kingdom to his great Mildmay Conferences who went away without that three-fold blessing which always seemed granted,—personal joy in the Lord, increase of desire for personal holiness; and great increase of zeal and power for work? These great blessings, together with more definite aims, and treasures of practical hints and suggestions for all imaginable branches of Christian work were taken back into hundreds of parishes, bearing untold fruit and golden results.

Would we have a glimpse of the inner life which resulted in such an outer life? Let us read the following hymns in their simple sequence, and we shall have it.

THE PALACE OF OUR KING.

And may I really tread
The palace of my King,
Gaze on the glory of His face,
And of His beauty sing?

I am not worthy, Lord!
Not worthy to draw near;
My feet are dusty with the way,
I hesitate—I fear!

"But wherefore tremble thus?
I washed thee clean, and white;
I decked thee with salvation's robe
Fairer than morning light!

"I hold thy hand in Mine,
And as I walk beside,
The pearly gates lift up their heads,
And for us open wide.

"They opened long ago,
Opened to let *Me* in,
When I, returning from the fight,
Had conquered death and sin.

"And they stand open still,
   Open, my child, for thee!
Then enter in with joyfulness,
   And use thy liberty."

Jesus! I *will* draw nigh,
   And in the "secret place,"
Behold the beauty of my Lord,
   And banquet on His grace.

THE RIVER OF LIFE.

Ere each morning breaketh,
   I would see Thy face,
Jesus! Precious Saviour!
   Jesus! King of Grace!

For my thirsty spirit.
   Longs to drink again
Of the living river
   Flowing through the plain.

Hark! how sweet its music
   As it dashes by,
Clear and fresh as ever,
   In its melody.

From the crystal city,
   From the throne on high,
It has leaped to succour
   Sinners lest they die!

Flowing where the desert
   Looks most parched and bare:
There its shining wavelets
   Sparkle everywhere!

We, with dying thousands,
   Would again partake
Of this crystal river—
   It our thirst can slake.

It the drooping pastures
    Can refresh and bless,
And with fragrant blossoms
    Clothe the wilderness!

Oh! Thou living Spirit,
    Give us of Thy dew:
Then our souls, like gardens,
    Will yield fruit anew!

"ONE LORD, ONE FAITH."

O Holy! Holy Father,
    O Christ ascended high,
O pure celestial Spirit,
    Eternal Trinity!
We, with Thy countless seraphs,
    We, with Thy saints in light,
Bow down in adoration,
    And praise Thee day and night.

One life pervades Thy ransomed,
    Within the golden gate,
And those who still are pilgrims,
    And for their glory wait.
The shouts of triumph yonder,
    The plaintive songs of earth,
Flow from the Spirit's presence;
    Both own a heavenly birth.

The precious blood of Jesus
    Is now within the veil—
Yonder Thy saints behold it,
    We too by it prevail!
Upon each shining forehead
    We read the Saviour's Name;
While we, now pressing forward,
    Bear on our brows the same.

Then teach us, Lord, to worship
With loving hearts to-day:
And whilst we sing Thy praises,
And learn in faith to pray,
Help us to feel our union
With all who know Thy Name,
And glory in Jehovah,
Unchangeably the same!

Let us seek the same close and joyful communion with our Lord Jesus, the same realization of union with Him, the same spirit of praise that cannot keep silence, the same clear and steadfast gaze of faith, which brings the "shining shore" "almost within sight," and then may we strive, not all in vain, to follow William Pennefather as he followed Christ.

Charlotte Elliott

Charlotte Elliott (1789–1871). F.R.H. wrote in a letter in 1869, "I hope you will get to know Charlotte Elliott; it is an honour from God to have had it given her, to write what she has written." (Letters by the Late Frances Ridley Havergal, *original book page 66, page 164 of Volume IV of the Havergal edition*)

II.

CHARLOTTE ELLIOTT'S HYMNS.

MISS Elliott's hymns are all heart-work; and whether written in the first, second, or third person we feel that she has lived every line; and this is why they touch other lives so magnetically. That which springs straight out of a living and beating heart is "poetry," and lives; that which does not is just "rhyming," and dies.

It may take many a year of living to produce a hymn which comes to the surface in one flash of thought, and is written in ten minutes. Even the writer does not know when the true making of that hymn began: perhaps far back in childhood, or among the "mists of the valley" which have been left behind years ago. Neither do our hymn-writers know how even to-day they are living out hymns unthought of, which will not be ready for the readiest pen till ten or twenty years have fed the hidden and growing germ. But some sudden touch of earth's tears or heaven's sunlight will set them free, and the growth of half a lifetime will blossom in an hour. And that is not the end, for there may be fruit unto life eternal to follow.

Such hymns are generally the simplest: every line is plain, and clear; but it is the clearness of depth, very different from the mystical muddiness of verse shallows, that have only been thought out, not lived out.

Such are Miss Elliott's hymns. Any one might have been written in half an hour, but more than half a century of patient suffering went to the making of them. "From early years she was more or less of an invalid," writes her sister, in the touching memorial* prefixed to her poems. It is rarely that a life so full of weakness and pain is prolonged for eighty-two years, before the silver cord is loosed.

But surely it was worth any suffering only to have written that one hymn, "Just as I am." Could any greater crown be set upon any life than to have been made God's messenger of peace to unknown thousands? We say thousands; but how could we count? All over the world that hymn has gone forth, and still goes—a bright, strong, heaven-sent hand, to lead sinful, sorrowful souls to the

* "Selections from the Poems of Charlotte Elliott. With a memoir by her sister."

the Lamb of God: some for the first time, others again and afresh. And the tale is not full yet; for it cannot die, as generations do. That refrain, "O Lamb of God, I come!" will ascend from many hearts in many lands and languages "till *He* come," and sorrow and sighing flee away. "It is one of those hymns which can never be sung or printed too often."

"JUST AS I AM."

Just as I am—without one plea,
But that Thy blood was shed for me,
And that Thou bidd'st me come to Thee—
    O Lamb of God, I come.

Just as I am—and waiting not
To rid my soul of one dark blot:
To Thee, whose blood can cleanse each spot—
    O Lamb of God, I come.

Just as I am—though tossed about
With many a conflict, many a doubt,
Fightings and fears within, without—
    O Lamb of God, I come.

Just as I am—poor, wretched, blind;
Sight, riches, healing of the mind,
Yea, all I need, in Thee to find—
    O Lamb of God, I come.

Just as I am—Thou wilt receive,
Wilt welcome, pardon, cleanse, relieve;
Because Thy promise I believe—
    O Lamb of God, I come.

Just as I am—Thy love unknown
Has broken every barrier down;
Now, to be Thine, yea, Thine alone—
    O Lamb of God, I come.

Just as I am—of that free love
The breadth, length, depth, and height to prove:
Here for a season, then above—
    O Lamb of God, I come.

It was not her doing. She only quietly placed it in "The Invalid's Hymn-book," probably with no thought of its passing beyond the lonely and shadowy rooms which that was to reach. But she had laid it somewhere else first. She took it as her own jewel of faith, tear-shining and true, out of her own heart, and laid it at the Saviour's feet. He took it up and sent it forth, as no human sending could have done, in the glorious strength of His blessing. One has said, what doubtless many have felt:—"I would rather have written that one hymn than all the sermons I ever preached."

Second only to this, which itself is perhaps second to none, is her touching hymn, "My God, my Father, while I stray."

"THY WILL BE DONE."

My God, My Father, while I stray,
Far from my home, on life's rough way,
Oh teach me from my heart to say,
> Thy will be done.

Though dark my path and sad my lot,
Let me be still and murmur not;
Or breathe the prayer Divinely taught,
> Thy will be done.

If Thou shouldst call me to resign
What most I prize, it ne'er was mine;
I only yield Thee what was Thine:
> Thy will be done.

Let but my fainting heart be blest
With Thy sweet Spirit for its guest,
My God, to Thee I leave the rest,—
> Thy will be done.

Renew my will from day to day,
Blend it with Thine, and take away
All that now makes it hard to say,
> Thy will be done.

Then, when on earth I breathe no more
The prayer oft mixed with tears before,
I'll sing upon a happier shore,
> Thy will be done.

There is a beautiful fitness in the fact that these two far-thrilling chords were struck by the same hand. For only the heart that has said, "Just as I am," can ever truly say, "Thy will be done." Only by the personal coming to the Lamb of God can we reach the quiet trust and love of the Father's will. Only through submissive acceptance of Christ's free salvation can we reach submissive acquiescence. Nay, we will not stop there, say rather restful rejoicing in God's sovereignty. The first hymn is the key to the second. For "that free love" is the essence of that "will."

Only in one point there seems to be a falling short, and that in the last verse, although lit up with the bright thought that,—

> "The prayer oft mixed with tears before,
> I'll *sing* upon a happier shore."

Why put off the singing? Why delay the change of sigh to song in uttering that *glorious* prayer; "Thy will be done"? "Understanding *what* the will of the Lord is." Yes, *what?* All, more than all that heart can desire, more than all our holiest, deepest longings have reached, all that Infinite Love can devise and bestow, all that Infinite Wisdom has planned, all that infinite Power will work in us and for us! Our salvation, our sanctification, our showing forth His glory, our joyful resurrection, our everlasting life, our being with Him and beholding His glory, and the countless and unspeakable blessings enfolded or linked with all this, *this* what we "ignorantly" ask when we pray those wonderful words which Jesus taught us; these are the true harmonies to that seemingly simple melody, "Thy will be done." When we search out in His Word what the will of the Lord is, and when we see that it is the very strength and action of His exceeding great love, then we do not wait till the "happier shore" is reached, but even here and now we *sing*, "Thy will be done."

But we must fill our specimen-glasses with other choice flowers from the same root whence grew "Just as I am" and "Thy will be done." Their heavenly fragrance is more noticeable than their poetic beauty, though this is by no means wanting. We will take the first two companion hymns. They complete each other—our faith and Christ's love, our clinging, His pleading.

"WE CLING TO THEE."

O Holy Saviour, Friend unseen,
Since on Thine arm Thou bidd'st us lean,
Help us throughout life's changing scene,
    By faith to cling to Thee.

Blest with this fellowship Divine,
Take what Thou wilt, we'll not repine;
Even as the branches to the vine,
    Our souls will cling to Thee.

Without a murmur we dismiss
Our former dreams of earthly bliss;
Our joy, our consolation this,
    Each hour to cling to Thee.

Though faith and hope may oft be tried,
We ask not, need not, aught beside;
So safe, so calm, so satisfied,
    The souls that cling to Thee!

They fear not Satan, nor the grave,
They know Thee near and strong to save,
Nor dread to cross e'en Jordan's wave,
    Because they cling to Thee.

Blest be our lot, whate'er befall!
What can disturb, or who appal,
While as our Strength, our Rock, our All,
    Saviour, we cling to Thee?

"OH, PLEAD FOR ME."

O Thou the contrite sinner's Friend
Who, loving, lov'st him to the end,
On this alone my hopes depend—
    That Thou wilt plead for me!

When, weary in the Christian race,
Far off appears my resting-place,
And fainting I mistrust Thy grace,
    Then, Saviour, plead for me!

When I have erred and gone astray
Afar from Thine and wisdom's way,
And see no glimmering guiding ray,
    Still, Saviour, plead for me!

When Satan, by my sins made bold,
Strives from Thy cross to loose my hold,
Then with Thy pitying arms enfold,
 And plead, oh, plead for me!

And when my dying hour draws near,
Darkened with anguish, guilt, and fear,
Then to my fainting sight appear,
 Pleading in heaven for me!

When the full light of heavenly day
Reveals my sins in dread array,
Say Thou hast washed them all away;
 Oh, say Thou plead'st for me!

Realization of the Lord Jesus Christ as a personal Saviour and Friend, personal love to Him, with a longing that rests in nothing short of His presence, seem to be the leading characteristics of Miss Elliott's writings. In one verse of another hymn she opens the very centre of her life and of her power; and the fulfilment of this great central desire was written upon her life and in her works, Jesus was a "living bright Reality" to her. How often we see such answers! When we converse about some special grace of the Spirit, and our friend says, with deep humility, "That is just what I want, just what I am asking continually for," how very often we feel, even if we do not say, "Why, that is the very thing you have!" And the very praying of this prayer will be a step towards its rich fulfilment.

JESUS KNOWN.

O Jesus, make Thyself to me
A living, bright Reality:
More present to faith's vision keen
Than any outward object seen;
More dear, more intimately nigh,
Than e'en the sweetest earthly tie!

It is pleasant to find that the long-questioned authorship of this helpful verse is now known.

"Faith's vision" is foretaste, but not fruition. And the sweeter the foretaste the deeper will be the longing for the fruition. When we have received and realized our Saviour's promise, "I will not leave you comfortless, I will come to you," then shines out that other "sure word" with nearer radiance and warmth, "I will come again and receive you unto Myself, that where I am there ye may be also." And so this hymn follows naturally upon the last-quoted verse.

"WITH CHRIST."

Let me be with Thee where Thou art,
  My Saviour, my eternal Rest!
Then only will this longing heart
  Be fully and for ever blest.

Let me be with Thee where Thou art,
  Thy unveiled glory to behold;
Then only will this wandering heart
  Cease to be faithless, treacherous, cold!

Let me be with Thee where Thou art,
  Where spotless saints Thy Name adore;
Then only will this sinful heart
  Be evil and defiled no more.

Let me be with Thee where Thou art,
  Where none can die,—where none remove!
Where life nor death my soul can part
  From Thy blest presence and Thy love!

We may remark here that Miss Elliott is exceptionally happy in refrain, and the short, simple, always telling words which she thus uses form the point to nearly all the swiftest and brightest arrows in her quiver. Most hymns leave a merely general impression; good memories quote whole verses, but others only retain a vague idea that it was "a very nice hymn." But once read, or, still better, once sung, the very essence of many of Miss Elliott's hymns is carried away in a single phrase, impossible to forget, and containing the one thought which all the rest unfolds or illustrates. "Just as I am" is a volume of divinity in four syllables. "We cling to Thee" and "Oh, plead for me," come back again and again; when a whole hymn, or even verse, would not be dwelt upon. "Let me be with Thee where Thou art" is all one's loving, and longing set to music in one bar.

Sometimes her refrain is taken from the most *musical,* as well as the most poetical Book that ever was written, as in this hymn:—

" IT IS I ; BE NOT AFRAID."

When waves of trouble round me swell;
　　My soul is not dismayed:
I hear a voice I know full well—
　　" 'Tis I; be not afraid."

When black the threatening skies appear,
　　And storms my path invade;
Those accents tranquillize each fear—
　　" 'Tis I; be not afraid."

There is a gulf that must be crossed;
　　Saviour, be near to aid!
Whisper, when my frail bark is tossed—
　　" 'Tis I; be not afraid."

There is a dark and fearful vale,
　　Death hides within its shade;
Oh, say, when flesh and heart shall fail—
　　" 'Tis I; be not afraid."

Tender experimental hymns were not the only outflow of this life of seclusion and suffering. Sometimes a clear trumpet-note rang out. And then, with that sensitive perception of metre which is analogous to an artist's choice of key in musical composition, she exchanged her usual meditative iambics for bright ringing trochaics. For instance, take the following:—

" WATCH AND PRAY."

" Christian! seek not yet repose";
Hear thy guardian angel say,
" Thou art in the midst of foes—
　　　　" Watch and pray!"

Principalities and powers,
Mustering their unseen array,
Wait for thy unguarded hours—
　　　　" Watch and pray!"

Gird thy heavenly armour on,
Wear it ever, night and day;
Ambushed lies the evil one—
"Watch and pray!"

Hear the victors who o'ercame:
Still they mark each warrior's way;
All, with one sweet voice, exclaim—
"Watch and pray!"

Hear, above all, hear thy Lord,
Him thou lovest to obey;
Hide within thy heart His word—
"Watch and pray!"

Watch, as if on that alone
Hung the issue of the day;
Pray that help may be sent down—
"Watch and pray!"

Or again this:—

"O FAINT AND FEEBLE HEARTED!"

O faint and feeble hearted!
Why thus cast down with fear?
Fresh aid shall be imparted,
Thy God unseen is near.

His eye can never slumber,
He marks thy cruel foes;
Observes their strength and number,
And all thy weakness knows.

Though heavy clouds of sorrow
Make dark thy path to-day,
There may shine forth to-morrow
Once more a cheering ray.

Doubts, griefs, and foes assailing,
Conceal heaven's fair abode;

Yet now faith's power prevailing
Should stay thy mind on God!

We have spoken of Miss Elliott's realizing faith; we find it joined, as such, faith always is, with earnest desire and effort to attain practical holiness. This comes out beautifully in,—

THE BELIEVER'S WANTS.

I want that adorning Divine
Thou only, my God, canst bestow;
I want in those beautiful garments to shine,
Which distinguish Thy household below.

I want every moment to feel
That Thy Spirit resides in my heart:
That His power is present to cleanse and to heal,
And newness of life to impart.

I want, oh, I want to attain
Some likeness, my Saviour, to Thee;
That longed-for resemblance once more to regain;
Thy comeliness put upon me.

I want to be marked for Thine own,
Thy seal on my forehead to wear;
To receive that " new name " on the mystic white stone,
Which none but Thyself can declare.

I want in Thee so to abide,
As to bring forth some fruit to Thy praise!
The branch which Thou prunest, though feeble and dried,
May languish, but never decays.

I want Thine own hand to unbind
Each tie to terrestrial things,—
Too tenderly cherished, too closely entwined,
Where my heart too tenaciously clings.

I want by my aspect serene,
My actions and words, to declare

That my treasure is placed in a country unseen,—
    That my heart's best affections are there.

I want, as a traveller, to haste
    Straight onward, nor pause on my way,
Nor forethought nor anxious contrivance to waste
    On the tent only pitched for a day.

I want,—and this sums up my prayer,—
    To glorify Thee till I die;
Then calmly to yield up my soul to Thy care,—
    And breathe out, in faith, my last sigh!"

A very striking means of giving effect and actuality to such desires is point-ed out in her hymn for "Saturday Morning." This gives a glimpse of the detail, so to speak, of her own practical efforts in this direction, and sets a very lovely and stimulating example of holy preparation for Sabbath blessing. Our Sun-days would often be very different, if our Saturdays thus "tuned with care each unseen chord within."

SATURDAY MORNING.

This is the day to tune with care
    Each unseen cord within:
Would we for Sabbaths well prepare,
    To-day we should begin.

Before the majesty of Heaven
    To-morrow we appear;
No honour half so great is given,
    Throughout man's sojourn here.

Yet if his heart be not prepared,
    His soul not meetly dressed,
In vain that honour will be shared,
    No smile will greet the guest.

We must beforehand lay aside
    Our own polluted dress,
And wear the robe of Jesu's bride
    His spotless righteousness.

We must forsake this world below,
    Forget all earthly things;
Strive with a seraph's love to glow,
    And soar on angel wings.

The altar must be cleansed to-day,
    Meet for the offered Lamb:
The wood in order we must lay,
    And wait to-morrow's flame.

Lord of the sacrifice we bring,
    To Thee our hopes aspire;
Our Prophet, our High Priest and King,
    Send down the sacred fire!

After such preparation of heart, what wonder that her Sunday morning song was so rich and full. The very page seems to glow with the holy sunshine lighting up her own heart. It is a golden litany; perhaps the brightest intercessory prayer ever written, as well as one of the most comprehensive.

THE SUN OF RIGHTEOUSNESS.

Thou glorious Sun of Righteousness,
    On this Day risen to set no more,
Shine on me now, to heal, to bless,
    With brighter beams than e'er before.

Shine on Thy work of grace within,
    On each celestial blossom there;
Destroy each bitter root of sin,
    And make Thy garden fresh and fair.

Shine on Thy pure eternal Word,
    Its mysteries to my soul reveal;
And whether read, remembered, heard,
    Oh, let it quicken, strengthen, heal!

Shine on the temples of Thy grace;
    In spotless robes Thy priests be clad;
There show the brightness of Thy Face,
    And make Thy chosen people glad.

Shine on those unseen things, displayed
    To faith's far penetrating eye;
And let their splendour cast a shade
    On every earthly vanity.

Shine in the hearts of those most dear,
    Disperse each cloud 'twixt them and Thee,
Their glorious heavenward prospects clear;
    "Light in Thy light," oh, let them see!

Shine on those friends for whom we mourn,
    Who know not yet Thy healing ray:
Quicken their souls and bid them turn
    To Thee, "the Life, the Truth, the Way."

Shine on those tribes no country owns,
    On Judah, once Thy dwelling-place;
"Thy servants think upon her stones,"
    And long to see her day of grace.

Shine on the missionary's home,
    Give him his heart's desire to see.
Collect thy scattered ones who roam;
    One fold, one Shepherd, let there be!

Shine, till Thy glorious beam shall chase
    The blinding film from every eye;
Till every earthly dwelling-place
    Shall hail the Dayspring from on high.

Shine on, shine on, Eternal Sun!
    Pour richer floods of life and light;
Till that bright Sabbath be begun,
    That glorious day which knows no night!

"That glorious day which knows no night" has begun for her. She does not regret now, she never did, that in early life she turned away from paths which had fair promise of earthly fame, and gave her talents all and entirely to Him who lent them to her. He gave her better things even in this life, I think *He always does*. And now, and henceforth, and for ever and ever, she has "the things which God hath prepared for them that love Him," and the never-ending fulfilment of her prayer, "Let me be with Thee where Thou art."

Her transition to this consummation was another page in the ever-filling records of the Saviour's faithfulness and tender love to His children. Her sister writes:—

"In the last years and days of her life—days of increased weakness and suffering—she was sustained and blessed with a sense of her Saviour's love and her Saviour's presence, and with a sure and abiding trust in Him ... The last manifestation of consciousness was on the morning of her death, when, on her sister repeating to her the text for the day, 'Thine eyes shall see the King in His beauty; they shall behold the land that is very far off,' she clasped her hands together; and as she raised her eyes to heaven, a beam came over her countenance which showed that she fully entered into the precious words, and was realizing the glorious vision she was so soon to behold. On the evening of that day, September 22d, 1871, without any apparent suffering or the slightest struggle, she fell asleep in Jesus."

SMYRNA. (Hymn Chant.)　　*Double Counterpoint.*　　[H. P. No. III.]

(3) INVITATIONS.

465　Rev. xxii. 17.　"*Whosoever will.*"　　Tune, Hymn Chant SMYRNA.　888, 6.

1 JUST as thou art, without one trace
　Of love, or joy, or inward grace,
Or meetness for the heavenly place,
　O guilty sinner, come!

2 Thy sins I bore on Calvary's tree!
The stripes, thy due, were laid on Me,
That peace and pardon might be free:
　O wretched sinner, come!

3 Burdened with guilt, wouldst thou be blest?
Trust not the world; it gives no rest:
I bring relief to hearts oppressed:
　O weary sinner, come!

4 Come, leave thy burden at the cross;
Count all thy gains but empty dross;
My grace repays all earthly loss:
　O needy sinner, come!

5 Come, hither bring thy boding fears,
Thy aching heart, thy bursting tears;
'Tis mercy's voice salutes thine ears,
　O trembling sinner, come!

6 "The Spirit and the Bride say, Come;"
Rejoicing saints re-echo, Come;
Who faints, who thirsts, who will, may come;
　Thy Saviour bids thee come!

Russell Sturgis Cook, 1850.

THYATIRA. (Hymn Chant.)　　[H. P. No. V.]

466　Jer. iii. 22.　"*Behold, we come unto Thee.*"
Tune, Hymn Chant THYATIRA.　Or BETHABARA.

1 JUST as I am—without one plea,
　But that Thy blood was shed for me,
And that Thou bidd'st me come to Thee,
　O Lamb of God, I come.

2 Just as I am—and waiting not
To rid my soul of one dark blot,
To Thee, whose blood can cleanse each spot,
　O Lamb of God, I come.

3 Just as I am—though tossed about
With many a conflict, many a doubt,
Fightings within, and fears without,
　O Lamb of God, I come.

4 Just as I am—poor, wretched, blind,
Sight, riches, healing of the mind,
Yea, all I need, in Thee to find,
　O Lamb of God, I come.

5 Just as I am—Thou wilt receive,
Wilt welcome, pardon, cleanse, relieve;
Because Thy promise I believe,
　O Lamb of God, I come.

6 Just as I am—(Thy love unknown
Has broken every barrier down)
Now, to be Thine, yea, Thine alone,
　O Lamb of God, I come.

7 Just as I am—of that free love
The breadth, length, depth, and height to prove,
Here for a season, then above,
　O Lamb of God, I come!

Charlotte Elliott, 1841.

WINCHESTER.　　[H. P. 46.]

467　Luke xiv. 22.　"*Yet there is room.*"　Tune WINCHESTER.　C. M.　Or KEDAR.

1 COME, sinner, to the gospel feast;
　Oh! come without delay:
For there is room in Jesu's breast
　For all who will obey.

2 There's room in God's eternal love
　To save thy precious soul!
Room in the Spirit's grace above
　To heal, and make thee whole.

3 There's room within the church redeemed
　With blood of Christ Divine.

Room in the white-robed throng convened,
　For that dear soul of thine.

4 There is room in heaven among the choir,
　And harps and crowns of gold,
And glorious palms of victory there,
　And joys that ne'er were told.

5 There's room around thy Father's board
　For thee and thousands more;
Oh! come, and welcome, to the Lord:
　Yea, come this very hour!

F. D. Huntingdon, 1843.

Known far more as a poet, F.R.H. was a rarely gifted pianist, composer, musician. She was the music editor of the hymnbook Songs of Grace and Glory, *preparing more than 1,100 tunes for publication in the hymnal. Most of the music had been composed by her father, William Henry Havergal, and posthumously arranged by Frances for the hymnal, but several tunes were composed by her, one of them being "Thyatira" (hymn 466). See page 8.*

From a Photograph by
The London Stereoscopic Company.

Dean Henry Alford (1810–1871).

III.

DEAN ALFORD'S HYMNS.

AMONG the "pleasant pictures" of our Church in the nineteenth century, one whose tints will be fresh and bright when more glaring colours are fading, is that of the gentle Christian scholar, patiently and lovingly toiling under the shadow of his grand cathedral. Patiently, for the work was long and great; lovingly, for it was sacred and sweet. We may imagine him now and then resting on his oars, and turning from his Greek Testament and his intensity of critical research, to solace himself with a short full musical setting of the spirit of the truths over whose letter he had been poring. Perhaps it was thus that this sweet Hymn on "Charity" came to him, and, through him, to the Church.

CHARITY.

Thou who on that wondrous journey
  Sett'st Thy Face to die:
By Thy holy meek example;
  Teach us Charity!

Thou who that dread cup of suffering
  Didst not put from Thee:
O most Loving of the loving,
  Give us Charity!

Thou who reignest, bright in glory,
  On God's throne on high:
Oh, that we may share Thy triumph—
  Grant us Charity!

Send us Faith that trusts Thy promise;
  Hope, with upward eye;
But more blest than both, and greater,
  Send us Charity!

Yet his life was not one-sided; and while, in addition to his theological work, he came forward on occasion as a champion of Protestant truth and facts, or as a clever and instructive contributor to periodicals, he did not refrain from coming "to the help of the Lord against the mighty," in the closer conflicts of "the work of an Evangelist." In this the same faithful perseverance which carried him through his great critical Commentary was not wanting; and our next Hymn shows him thus at once working and waiting for his Master.

LABOUR FOR CHRIST.

"All the night and nothing taken"—
　　How shall we let down the net?
All our steadfast hopes are shaken,
　　Every scheme with failure met;
　　　　Though we speak the Message clear,
　　　　Yet the sinner will not hear.

"All the night and nothing taken"—
　　And the hours be speeding by;
Is the chosen flock forsaken?
　　Is no Master standing nigh?
　　　　Nought is found among the band
　　　　But faint heart and weary hand.

Still, though night may pass in sorrow,
　　And no guiding star appear,
Sounds the promise for the morrow
　　From the Master standing near:
　　　　"Ye shall find": then hopeful yet
　　　　At His word we loose the net!

Dean Alford's contributions to hymnology are not widely known, though his Hymnal, "The Year of Praise," containing many of his own hymns, is far more excellent than some which are far more popular. His quaint and beautiful Baptismal Hymn—

"In token that thou shalt not fear
　　Christ crucified to own"—

written so early as 1832, is, however, so generally adopted that it may be considered as one of our standard Church hymns.

His Hymn for the last Sunday after Trinity, dated 1867, supplied a want in our Church Hymnology. Its chastened tone of grateful retrospect and trustful anticticipation harmonize well with the quiet November Sunday which closes the privileges of our ecclesiastical year. The line which leads up into the doxology—

"And then our darkness with Thy glory fill"—

is singularly perfect, not only in its musical balancing of vowel sounds and accents, but in its uplifting suggestiveness of expression; while its position in the Hymn, as a shining, stepping-stone from prayer to praise, enhances its value and beauty.

" O SEND OUT THY LIGHT AND THY TRUTH."

Our year of grace is wearing to its close,
    Its autumn storms are louring from the sky;
    Shine on us with Thy light; O God Most High,
Abide with us where'er our pathway goes,
Our Guide in toil, our Guardian in repose.

All through the months hath beamed Thy cheering light,
    From Bethlehem's Day-Star waxing ever on:
    Through every cloud Thy Blessèd Sun hath shone.
Earth may be dark to them that walk by sight,
But for Thy Church the day is always bright.

Light us in life, that we may see Thy will,
    The track Thine hand hath ordered for our way:
    Light us, when shadows gather o'er our day:
Shine on us in that passage lone and chill,
And then our darkness with Thy glory fill.

Praise be to God from earth's remotest coast,
    From lands and seas, and each created race:
    Praise from the worlds His hand hath launched in space:
Praise from the Church, and from the heavenly host:
Praise to the Father, Son, and Holy Ghost.

In sparkling contrast to the subdued tone and grave measure of the foregoing stands a Hymn on "The Coming Glory," which vividly realizes "things not
seen as yet."

It is a hymn to tune up the voices as well as the hearts of any congregation.
It must be a hopeless choir indeed which could possibly get "flat" in it, and a
hopeless congregation indeed which would not be stirred up to join right heart-
ily. It is so bright so clear, so *near-bringing;* one sees the dazzling whiteness of
the robes, and the glory of the opening gates; the very ear is filled with the "rush
of hallelujahs" and the "ringing of a thousand harps."

It is a manly hymn of heaven, and the faith that echoes it will not be the
faith of mere desire and far-off anticipation, but of noble strife and following.
And the third verse adds to the reality of the vision, by its touch upon the things
that are so close to us.

THE COMING GLORY

Ten thousand times ten thousand,
   In sparkling raiment bright,
The armies of the ransomed saints
   Throng up the steeps of light:
'Tis finished—all is finished,
   Their fight with death and sin;
Fling open wide the golden gates,
   And let the victors in!

What rush of Hallelujahs
   Fills all the earth and sky!
What ringing of a thousand harps
   Bespeaks the triumph nigh!
O day, for which creation
   And all its tribes were made:
O joy! for all its former woes
   A thousandfold repaid.

Oh then what raptured greetings
   On Canaan's happy shore!
What knitting severed friendships up
   Where partings are no more!

Then eyes with joy shall sparkle
That brimmed with tears of late:
No longer orphans fatherless,
Nor widows desolate.

Ten thousand times ten thousand,
In sparkling raiment bright.
The armies of the ransomed saints
Throng up the steeps of light:
'Tis finished—all is finished,
Their fight with death and sin;
Fling open wide the golden gates,
And let the victors in!

Those " raptured greetings " were not so very far off when this bright hymn was written. But one life-wish was yet unfulfilled—that he might " stand within thy gates, O Jerusalem." It was all planned, that thoughtful, sacred journey; undertaken not for his own refreshment and enjoyment alone, but for the enrichment of many an untravelled Christian student. But the Master had planned a " better thing " for His weary servant; and after a short passage of suffering, the feet that never trod the earthly Zion entered " that great city, the holy Jerusalem," to " go no more out."

99 Ps. xxxiv. 1. *"I will bless the Lord at all times."* Tune EDEN. C. M. Or WINCHESTER.

1 LORD ! I would delight in Thee,
   And on Thy care depend;
   To Thee in every trouble flee,
   My best—my only Friend !

2 When all created streams are dried,
   Thy fulness is the same ;
   May I with this be satisfied,
   And glory in Thy name !

3 Why should the soul a drop bemoan,
   Who has a fountain near ;
   A fountain which will ever run
   With water sweet and clear ?

4 No good in creatures can be found,
   But may be found in Thee ;

I must have all things, and abound,
   While God is God to me

5 Oh that I had a stronger faith,
   To look within the veil ;
   To credit what my Saviour saith,
   Whose word can never fail !

6 He that has made my heaven secure,
   Will here all good provide ;
   While Christ is rich, can I be poor ?
   What can I want beside ?

7 O Lord ! I cast my care on Thee,
   I triumph and adore :
   Henceforth my great concern shall be
   To love and please Thee more !

   John Ryland, D.D., 1777.

[H. P. 149.]

VIENNA.

100 Ps. xxxi. 15. *" My times are in Thy hand."* Tune VIENNA. 77, 77.

1 SOVEREIGN Ruler of the skies,
   Ever gracious, ever wise !
   All my times are in Thy hand,
   All events at Thy command.

2 His decree who formed the earth,
   Fixed my first and second birth ;
   Parents, native place, and time,
   All appointed were by Him.

3 He that formed me in the womb,
   He shall guide me to the tomb ;
   All my times shall ever be
   Ordered by His wise decree.

4 Times of sickness, times of health ;
   Times of penury and wealth ;
   Times of trial and of grief ;
   Times of triumph and relief.

5 Times the tempter's power to prove ;
   Times to taste a Saviour's love ;
   All must come, and last, and end,
   As shall please my heavenly Friend.

6 Plagues and deaths around me fly ;
   Till He bids, I cannot die ;
   Not a single shaft can hit,
   Till the God of love thinks fit.

7 O Thou Gracious, Wise, and Just,
   In Thy hands my life I trust !
   Have I somewhat dearer still ?
   I resign it to Thy will.

8 May I always own Thy hand—
   Still to the surrender stand ;
   Know that Thou art God alone :
   I and mine are all Thine own.

9 Thee at all times will I bless ;
   Having Thee I all possess :
   How can I bereavèd be,
   Since I cannot part with Thee !

   John Ryland, D.D., 1777.

EUODIAS.

[H. P. 255.]

101 2 Kings iv. 26. *" It is well."*
   Tune EUODIAS. 8 4, 8 4, 8 8 8 4.

1 THROUGH the love of God our
        Saviour,
   All will be well ;
   Free and changeless is His favour,
   All, all is well !
   Precious is the blood that healed us ;
   Perfect is the grace that sealed us :
   Strong the hand stretched out to
        All must be well ! [shield us ;

2 Though we pass through tribulation,
   All will be well ;
   Ours is such a full salvation,
   All, all is well !
   Happy, still in God confiding ;
   Fruitful, if in Christ abiding ;
   Holy, through the Spirit's guiding :
   All must be well !

3 We expect a bright to-morrow,
   All will be well ;
   Faith can sing through days of sorrow,
   All, all is well !
   On our Father's love relying,
   Jesus every need supplying,
   Both in living and in dying,
   All must be well !   *Mary Bowly, 1847.*

This is page 41 of Songs of Grace and Glory. *Published in 1880 (the year after her death), with nearly all the music prepared by F.R.H., the finalized hymnal had 434 pages of hymns, more than 1,100 scores of music. Volume V of the Havergal edition presents music composed by Frances and by her father, William Henry Havergal. F.R.H. composed "Euodias," the music for hymn 101. See pages 39–40 of this book.*

Drawn by T. D. SCOTT, from a Photograph.   52

Bishop Wordsworth (1807–1885).

IV.

BISHOP WORDSWORTH'S HYMNS.

O UR next set of "Specimen-Glasses" shall contain Hymns by Christopher
Wordsworth, Bishop of Lincoln—Hymns which reflect the heart of a
joyful saint, together with a frequent touch of poetic glow, and a beauty of form
and language worthy of the famous name he bears.

No characteristic of Bishop Wordsworth's Hymns is more striking than their
fulness of Scriptural teaching. They are rich in typical suggestion, and some are
as a brilliant picture-gallery of Old Testament story, on which one concentrated
ray of New Testament sunlight is made to fall. Take, for instance, one of his Easter Hymns, and mark how much historical and doctrinal teaching is compressed
into its eight verses, while the mastery over a difficult metre adds to the sense of
masculine power which we feel in this condensed commentary.

RESURRECTION TEACHING.

In thy glorious Resurrection,
Lord, we see a world's erection:
    Man in Thee is glorified.
Bliss, for which the patriarchs panted,
Joys, by holy psalmists chanted,
    Now in Thee are verified!

Oracles of former ages,
Veiled in dim prophetic pages,
    Now lie open to the sight;
Now the types which glimmered darkling
In the twilight gloom, are sparkling
    In the blaze of noonday light.

Isaac from the wood is risen;
Joseph issues from the prison;
    See the Paschal Lamb which saves;
Israel through the sea is landed,

Pharaoh and his hosts are stranded,
And o'erwhelmèd in the waves.

See the cloudy pillar leading,
Rock refreshing, manna feeding;
    Joshua fights and Moses prays;
See the lifted wave-sheaf, cheering
Pledge of harvest-fruits appearing,
    Joyful dawn of happy days.

Samson see at night uptearing
Gaza's brazen gates, and bearing
    To the top of Hebron's hill;
Jonah comes from stormy surges,
From his three-days' grave emerges
    Bids beware of coming ill.

So Thy Resurrection's glory
Sheds a light on ancient story;
    And it casts a forward ray,
Beacon-light of solemn warning;
To the dawn of that great Morning,
    Ushering in the Judgment day.

Ever since Thy death and rising
Thou the nations art baptising
    In Thy death's similitude;
Dead to sin and ever dying,
And our members mortifying,
    May we walk with life renewed!

Forth from Thy first Easter going,
Sundays are for ever flowing
    Onward to a boundless sea;
Lord, may they for Thee prepare us,
On a holy river bear us
    To a calm eternity!

Another of Bishop Wordsworth's Easter Hymns appeals rather to spiritual than intellectual sympathy, and its teaching, not less full, will be more widely and deeply felt. In this we are led on by a loving and fervent hand into an inner and more glorious temple: the glow of personal faith and love breathes around; the Risen Lord Himself is "the Light thereof"; and we are led to recognise and rejoice in the mystery and glory of "the power of His Resurrection," in which we, too, have part; for "Christ is risen, *we* are risen!" Those who have not had the privilege of joining in this Hymn on an Easter morning can have little idea of its stirring and elevating power. Old associations are very strong in touching and arousing the heart, but truths of God, deep and grand and full, and clothed in such verse, are stronger; and with all our love for the old strains familiar from childhood, we cannot help feeling that in some cases "the new wine" is better than the old.

"CHRIST IS RISEN: WE ARE RISEN."

Hallelujah! Hallelujah! Hearts to heaven and voices raise!
Sing to God a hymn of gladness, sing to God a hymn of praise!
He who on the Cross a victim for the world's salvation bled,
Jesus Christ, the King of Glory, now is risen from the dead.

Now the iron bars are broken, Christ from death to life is born,
Glorious life, and life immortal, on this holy Easter morn:
Christ has triumphed, and we conquer by His mighty enterprise.
We with Him to life eternal by His Resurrection rise.

Christ is risen, Christ the first-fruits of the holy harvest field,
Which will all its full abundance at His second coming yield;
Then the golden ears of harvest will their heads before Him wave,
Ripened by His glorious sunshine, from the furrows of the grave.

Christ is risen: we are risen! Shed upon us heavenly grace,
Rain and dew and gleams of glory from the brightness of Thy Face:
That we, Lord, with hearts in heaven, here on earth may fruitful be,
And by angel-hands be gathered, and be ever safe with Thee.

Hallelujah! Hallelujah! Glory be to God on high!
Hallelujah! to the Saviour, who has gained the victory;
Hallelujah! to the Spirit, Fount of Love and Sanctity;
Hallelujah! Hallelujah! to the Triune Majesty!

The characteristics of Bishop Wordsworth's two Easter Hymns already quoted are grandly combined in an unparalleled Ascension Hymn, beyond question the finest hymn in our language for that great Festival.

THE ASCENSION.

See the Conqueror mounts in triumph, see the King in royal state,
Riding on the clouds His chariot, to His heavenly palace gate;
Hark, the choirs of angel voices joyful Hallelujahs sing,
And the portals high are lifted to receive their heavenly King.

Who is this that comes in glory, with the trump of jubilee?
Lord of battles, God of armies, He has gained the victory;
He who on the Cross did suffer, He who from the grave arose,
He has vanquished sin and Satan, He by death has spoiled His foes.

While He raised His hands in blessing, He was parted from His friends;
While their eager eyes behold Him, He upon the clouds ascends;
He who walked with God, and pleased Him, preaching truth, and doom to
    come,
He, our Enoch, is translated to His everlasting home.

Now our heavenly Aaron enters, with His blood, within the veil;
Joshua now is come to Canaan, and the kings before Him quail!
Now He plants the tribes of Israel in their promised resting-place;
Now our great Elijah offers double portion of His grace.

Thou hast raised our human nature in the clouds to God's right hand:
There we sit in heavenly places, there with Thee in glory stand;
Jesus reigns, adored by angels; man with God is on the throne;
Mighty Lord, in Thine Ascension we by faith behold our own!

Holy Ghost, Illuminator, shed Thy beams upon our eyes;
Help us to look up with Stephen, and to see, beyond the skies,
Where the Son of Man in glory standing is at God's right hand,
Beckoning on His martyr army, succouring His faithful band.

See Him, who is gone before us heavenly mansions to prepare;
See Him, who is ever pleading for us with prevailing prayer;
See Him, who with sound of trumpet and with His angelic train,
Summoning the world to Judgment, on the clouds will come again!

Lift us up from earth to heaven, give us wings of faith and love,
Gales of holy aspirations wafting us to realms above;
That, with hearts and minds uplifted, we with Christ our Lord may dwell,
Where He sits enthroned in glory, in His heavenly citadel.

So at last, when He appeareth, we from out our graves may spring.
With our youth renewed like eagles, flocking round our heavenly King,
Caught up on the clouds of heaven, and may meet Him in the air,
Rise to realms where He is reigning, and may reign for ever there.

Glory be to God the Father; glory be to God the Son,
Dying, risen, ascending for us, who the heavenly realm has won;
Glory to the Holy Spirit, to one God in Persons Three,
Glory both in earth and heaven, glory, endless glory be.

It may be objected that this magnificent Hymn is too long for singing. Try
it! and see if the interest and richness of thought do not carry you on farther
than you expected. For Church use, the German plan of dividing a long hymn,
by singing a part before and a part after the sermon, is often found practically
useful and pleasing, and tends to that unity of the services which is too often lost
when the hymns selected have no connection either with each other or with the
sermon. In this manner congregations may be both instructed and delighted
with this beautiful epitome of Ascension teaching and Ascension gladness.

A contrast to the foregoing is found in a sweet, simple, and spiritual em-
bodiment of the leading petitions of the fifty-first Psalm. Few, if any, Lenten
hymns equal this touching prayer: or will be found more helpful to the penitent
"in sorrow and distress."

"IN SORROW AND DISTRESS."

In sorrow and distress,
To Thee, O Lord, we fly;
In penitential lowliness
To Thee for mercy cry.

Mercy, oh, mercy, Lord;
From Thee we have our breath:
We read it written in Thy Word,
"God willeth not your death:

"God gave His only Son
Your sins to take away;
And God's dear Son to heaven is gone
On your behalf to pray."

By Thine own love we plead,
  Oh, hearken to our prayer;
By Him, who for our sins did bleed,
  Spare us, O Father, spare.

Our drooping minds refresh
  With showers of heavenly dew;
For hearts of stone give hearts of flesh—
  Renew us, Lord, renew.

Comfort and make us whole
  With Thy free Spirit's grace;
Lift up, O Lord, upon our soul
  The lustre of Thy face.

With Jesu's white robe hide
  Our manifold offence;
And cleanse with blood from Jesu's side
  Our tears of penitence.

Constrain us to abhor
  The sins that made Him grieve,
And ne'er to tempt the Spirit more
  Our thankless hearts to leave.

Make us, O Lord, to tread
  The path which Jesus trod;
Which Him from earth in triumph led
  To the right hand of God.

So with the saints in heaven,
  May we sing praise to Thee,
For peace restored, and sins forgiven—
  To all eternity!

Another of Bishop Wordsworth's hymns furnishes an example of quaint typical thought:—

SCRIPTURAL TYPES.

Upon the sixth day of the week
  The first man had his birth,

In God's own image bright and pure
    Created from the earth,

Upon the sixth day of the week
    The Second Adam died,
And by the Second Adam's death
    Man was revivified.

Upon the seventh day of the week
    God from His works did rest,
And on that holy Sabbath day
    The works of God were blessed.

Upon the seventh day of the week
    Christ in the grave did rest.
The grave is now a holy place;
    A Sabbath for the blest.

By tasting the forbidden tree
    Man fell in Paradise;
Upon the tree Christ tasted death,
    And by His death we rise.

Christ in a garden buried lay,
    Which spring-flowers did adorn;
And there our Resurrection bloomed
    On the bright Easter morn.

The grave itself a garden is,
    Where loveliest flowers abound,
For Christ our amaranthine Life
    Sprang from the holy ground.

He by the Spirit once was born
    Pure from the Virgin's womb,
And by the Spirit once again
    Born from the virgin tomb.

Oh, give us grace to die to sin,
    That we, O Lord, may have
A holy, happy rest with Thee,
    A Sabbath in the grave.

Oh, may we buried be with Thee,
And with Thee, Lord, arise
To an eternal Easter-day
Of glory in the skies!

The following Evening Hymn deserves a place by the side of Lyte's "Abide
with me," and Keble's "Sun of my soul."

EVENING HYMN.

The day is gently sinking to a close,
Fainter and yet more faint the sunlight grows;
O Brightness of Thy Father's glory, Thou
Eternal Light of Light, be with us now;
Where Thou art present, darkness cannot be:
Midnight is glorious noon, O Lord, with Thee.

Our changeful lives are ebbing to an end,
Onward to darkness and to death we tend;
O Conqueror of the grave, be Thou our Guide,
Be Thou our Light in death's dark eventide;
Then in our mortal hour will be no gloom,
No sting in death, no terror in the tomb.

Thou, who in darkness walking didst appear
Upon the waves, and Thy disciples cheer,
Come, Lord, in lonesome days, when storms assail,
And earthly hopes and human succours fail
When all is dark, may we behold Thee nigh,
And hear Thy voice, "Fear not, for it is I."

The weary world is mouldering to decay,
Its glories wane, its pageants fade away:
In that last sunset, when the stars shall fall,
May we arise, awakened by Thy call,
With Thee, O Lord, for ever to abide
In that blest day which has no eventide!

V.

HYMNS BY CHARITIE LEES SMITH AND MARY BOWLY.

"Now there are diversities of gifts, but the same Spirit." We do not look for cedars among the beds of lilies. We do not ask for masculine grandeur and concentrated force from the handmaids of the Lord. But we expect, and we find, gifts not less precious, and power not less real, though of a different kind.

I have often been struck with the fact that the soft and apparently far less powerful tones of a harp are more penetrating, and vibrate to greater distances in the open air, than those of other instruments which overpower them when near. A simple flute often reaches both ear and soul with a peculiar thrill, through all the dazzling sounds of a great orchestra. These seem the nearest analogies to good hymns by lady writers. They have a harp-like soul-penetration, and a flute-like individuality beyond others. They are

"Tender in their strength,
And in their very tenderness are strong."

Our first Hymn, by a clergyman's daughter, Charitie Lees Smith, was written in the flush and fervour of coming "out of darkness into marvellous light," during the great awakenings of 1859–60 in Ireland,—the very first chord of a newly-strung harp. It is no great wonder that thousands, who know nothing about its origin, should have instinctively caught it up as the true expression of their own feelings at the same great crisis, whenever and wherever occurring.

ASPIRATION.

Oh, for the robes of whiteness!
Oh, for the tearless eyes!
Oh, for the glorious brightness
Of the unclouded skies!

Oh, for the no more weeping
Within that land of love,

The endless joy of keeping
The bridal feast above!

Oh, for the bliss of flying,
My Risen Lord to meet!
Oh, for the rest of lying
For ever at His feet!

Oh, for the hour of seeing
My Saviour face to face!
The hope of ever being
In that sweet meeting-place!

Jesus! Thou King of Glory,
I soon shall dwell with Thee;
I soon shall sing the story
Of Thy great love to me.

Meanwhile, my thoughts shall enter
E'en now before Thy throne:
That all my love may centre
In Thee, and Thee alone.

Calmer, riper, and maturer are the hymns of Mary Bowly. They are not the hymns of a young Christian, but evidently of one who has found "grace for grace," and gone "from strength to strength"; whose faith is buttressed by knowledge, and whose confidence and joy have been not merely tested, but deepened by experience. Theirs is the glow which succeeds to the flame, the daylight which follows the dawn-flush. They are not a mere outflow of poetical fervour and fancy, but every line, generally speaking, contains some distinct reality of Scripture truth or Christian experience. Take, for instance, a hymn fitly adapted for the opening of a New Year, entitled:—

"IT IS WELL."

Through the love of God our Saviour,
All will be well;
Free and changeless is His favour:
All, all is well!

Precious is the blood that healed us;
Perfect is the grace that sealed us;
Strong the hand stretched out to shield us;
          All must be well!

Though we pass through tribulation,
          All will be well;
Ours is such a full salvation:
          All, all is well!
Happy, still in God confiding,
Fruitful, if in Christ abiding,
Holy, through the Spirit's guiding:
          All must be well!

We expect a bright to-morrow:
          All will be well;
Faith can sing through days of sorrow,
          All, all is well!
On our Father's love relying,
Jesus every need supplying.
Both in living and in dying,
          All must be well!

Equally rich in Scriptural teaching is the following;—

DIVINE LOVE.

Holy Father! we address Thee—
          Loved in Thy belovèd Son;
Holy Son of God, we bless Thee:
          Boundless grace hath made us one.
Holy Spirit, aid our songs:
This glad work to Thee belongs.

Wondrous was Thy love, O Father!
          Wondrous Thine, O Son of God!
Vast the love that bruised and wounded,
          Vast the love that bore the rod;
Holy Spirit, still reveal,
How those stripes alone can heal.

Gracious Father, Thy good pleasure
   Is to love us as Thy Son:
Meting out the self-same measure,
   Since Thou seest us as one.
Blessèd Jesus! loved are we,
As the Father loveth Thee.

Hallelujah! we are hasting
   To our Father's house above;
By the way our souls are tasting
   Rich and everlasting love;
In Jehovah is our boast,
Father, Son, and Holy Ghost!

The bright assurance of faith expressed in these hymns is the simple absolute rest of the soul in the infinite and absolute love of the Father in His Son Jesus Christ. It is the simple taking of those wonderful words as absolutely true—"Thou hast loved them, as Thou hast loved Me."

VI.

HYMNS OF JOY.

OH, the rubbish calling itself poetry that Christian girls sing to Christian friends when asked to give pleasure by "a little music"!

"One can't very well sing just a *hymn,* you know!"

And why not? Just *try* singing "Rejoice in the Lord," and I am not anxious as to the result.

"But sacred music does not suit my voice," says my friend.

Very likely secular songs are a little more showy than sacred ones, but your object is not show or display. Besides, you are in the habit of singing the former, and that makes more difference than you would suppose till you have given the latter an equally fair trial.

Let us fairly balance the matter. Although the average of sacred music is really far superior to secular, we will suppose it to be merely equal. But then, what have we in addition? First, the added value of the words, with the opportunity of winning and witnessing for Jesus by them. Secondly, the added power of heart and love and conscience all thrown into the scale when we are really " singing for Jesus," which cannot fail to give truer and more touching expression than any singing-master can teach. And thirdly, and chiefly, we may expect and we find the actual help and power and presence of the Master Himself, and surely that outweighs all else.

One of the most experienced trainers of professional singers listened critically to a song rendered in this spirit. He paused and hesitated, and then said emphatically, "You have not much voice, but, *mark my words,* you will always be able to beat anybody with four times your voice." This anecdote may give a little practical encouragement in the matter.

Now for a right joyous Spring and Easter call to rise up and rejoice. Only let it be sung, not read: sung with the heart and sung with the voice. It is from the gifted pen of Marianne Farningham Hearn.

REJOICE IN THE LORD.

Rejoice in the Lord! there is light in the dwelling,
    And peace in the spirit, where Christ is the Guest;
And surely the chorus might always be swelling
    Around the glad threshold which Jesus has blessed.

Rejoice in the Lord! He will scatter the sadness
    That broods o'er the sanctified home of His friends;
And days as they pass will be radiant with gladness,
    Where prayer from the family altar ascends.

Rejoice in the Lord! the fresh flowerets are springing
    In fragrance and beauty to gladden thy way:
The Father of mercies His largess is flinging—
    New tokens of love for each newly born day.

Rejoice in the Lord! He is tenderly leading
    Each step that His wisdom requires thee to take;
And He will supply all the strength thou art needing,
    Who loveth for ever and will not forsake.

Rejoice in the Lord! there is joy for thee ever,
    If thou in thy lifetime belongest to Him;
A bond—all of love—which no change can e'er sever,
    A sun o'er thy head which no storm-cloud can dim.

Rejoice in the Lord! He awaits thee in heaven,
    With myriads who make His light service their choice;
And shortly the robe and the crown will be given
    To thee! Then, believer, oh! always rejoice!

As a specimen of hymns of joy and gladness for the young, one by Miss Threlfall, originally written some years ago as a Whitsuntide hymn for *Home Words,* has become in the fullest sense "a standard hymn." It is one of the brightest and most graceful hymns for the little ones that can adorn any collection.

"HOSANNA."

Hosanna! loud hosanna!
 The little children sang;
Through pillared court and temple
 The lovely anthem rang;
To Jesus, who had blessed them,
 Close folded to His breast,
The children sang their praises,
 The simplest and the best.

From Olivet they followed,
 'Mid that exultant crowd,
The victor palm-branch waving,
 And shouting clear and loud;
Bright angels joined the chorus,
 Beyond the cloudless sky—
"Hosanna in the highest:
 Glory to God on high!"

Fair leaves of silvery olive
 They strewed upon the ground,
Whilst Salem's circling-mountains
 Echoed the joyful sound:
The Lord of men and angels
 Rode on in lowly state,
Nor scorned that little children
 Should on His bidding wait.

"Hosanna in the highest!"
 That ancient song *we* sing;
For Christ is our Redeemer,
 The Lord of heaven our King.
Oh! may we ever praise Him,
 With heart, and life, and voice,
And in His blissful presence,
 Eternally rejoice!

VII.

HYMNS FOR SUFFERERS.

CHRISTIAN song is very dear to sufferers, and its ministry seldom fails to bring home the heart-cheer of some Bible truth or promise.

Thoughts of four sweet singers, Jennette Threlfall, Jane E. Joy, Mary Shekleton, and Mrs. Crewdson, are thus specially linked with 2 Corinthians 1:4: "Who comforteth us in all our tribulation, that we may be able to comfort them which are in trouble, by the comfort wherewith we ourselves are comforted of God."

One hymn by the first-named writer, perhaps better known by her long-used initials, "J. T.," has brought more "strong consolation" to invalids within the range of our own knowledge than any other uninspired words. We could tell of one sufferer under whose weary pillow that hymn was kept for two years of incessant pain; and of another who drew comfort from it almost daily for eleven years. Never once has the gift of these simple lines failed to awaken grateful response.

"Written during long and dangerous illness," says the heading to these verses in the author's volume of poems. "Written," but by another hand, when the physical strength had ebbed so low, that a faint whisper of line by line, dictating thus to a bending ear, was all that it could do.

Surely strength was here made perfect in weakness, in this outflow of the precious ointment of sweet service from the broken alabaster of the suffering frame. It is indeed "heart to heart," and its power lies in its reality.

We give it in full, hoping thus to extend its ministry of comfort.

"THEY WATCHED HIM THERE."

I think of Thee, O Saviour!
And count affliction gain,
If aught of suffering aid me
To realise Thy pain.

I think of Thee, O Saviour!
    And bless the chastening rod,
Conforming to Thine image,
    Thou chastened Son of God.

I think of Thee, O Saviour!
    My trial hath been long;
But night hath not seemed weary,
    For Thou hast been my song.

I think of Thee, O Saviour!
    When loving voices seek,
In tender tones of pity,
    Their sympathy to speak.

How different the revilings
    Which Thou didst bear for me;
The scorn, the taunts, the tumult,
    Sounding on Calvary!

I think of Thee, when brightly
    The Father's love doth shine,
Lighting as with a sunbeam
    This fainting heart of mine.

Oh, then, Thy cry of wailing
    Seems sounding in mine ear;
God's billows rolling o'er Thee,
    Forsaken in Thy fear.

More often still, my Saviour,
    I meditate of Thee,
When by my couch some dear one
    Sits watching silently:

For no fond ear bent sadly
    To list *Thy* parting breath;
The stranger and the foeman
    Sat watching for *Thy* death.

Uncheered, unmitigated
    The cup to Thee was given;—

My every pain is lightened
   By love from earth and heaven.

Each feverish fancy granted
   Almost before expressed;
Luxuriously pillowed,
   And soothingly caressed.

Oh! 'tis well-nigh presumption
   In sufferings light as mine,
To speak, my stricken Saviour,
   Of fellowship with Thine!

But by the reckless aching,
   Which findeth no relief;
And by the hidden conflict
   With sin and unbelief:—

By life's slow weary ebbing,
   By death so long delayed,
By the dark grave familiar,
   Because so oft surveyed:—

By each of these, my Saviour,
   I learn to realise,
Though but in feeblest measure,
   Thy dying agonies.

My sufferings no atonement
   For sin could make to God;
Alone, of all the people,
   Thou hast the winepress trod.

So there is nought of anger
   In this my Father's stroke;
He is but gently teaching
   My neck to bear Thy yoke.

And it is joy, my Saviour,
   A blessèd joy, to think
The cup I am but tasting,
   Thou didst vouchsafe to drink.

I would press closer to Thee;
    A heavier cross would bear:
So I might better know Thee,
    And more Thy Spirit share.

It was Thy cloud which led me
    All through the joyous day;
But now the fiery pillar
    Is shining on my way.

And I shall better praise Thee,
    Seeing Thee thus by night,
Than if the desert pathway
    Had all been tracked in light.

Soon, as Thou overcamest,
    I too shall overcome;
And bless the love which kept me
    So long away from home.

I had been lost for ever,
    Hadst Thou not thought on me;
Cold is my heart, and selfish;
    Yet, Lord, I think on Thee!

VIII.

HYMNS FOR SUFFERERS—*(Continued).*

H ERE is a happy "song in the night" by one whose initials, "J. E. J." are familiar to the readers of most of our leading religious periodicals. Solitary "hours of darkness" have borne much fruit of brightness for other lonely watchers. What the Master hath told her in darkness, that she hath spoken in the light. Days alone with His presence and His Word have enabled her to bring forth things "new and old" for others: and thus perhaps the chief characteristic of her verse is the amount of Scriptural illustration and allusion always enriching it.

LIGHT IN DARKNESS.

("Lux lucet in tenebras."—*Motto of the Waldensian Church*).

In an hour of darkness,
　Through the opened skies,
Fell on ears of mortals
　Heavenly melodies.

In an hour of darkness
　Israel's hope was born;—
Then arose "the Day-Star,"
　Herald of the morn.

In an hour of darkness
　Israel's Saviour died;—
Sprang our light and gladness
　From the Crucified.

In an hour of darkness
　Open flew the cave;
Jesu's Resurrection
　Proved Him strong to save.

In an hour of darkness—
    Ere Gethsemane
And the Cross—our Master
    Said "Remember Me!"

In an hour of darkness
    Heard His faithful few
Those sweet words of blessing:
    "Peace be unto you!"

In an hour of darkness,
    Mystic, deep, and wide:—
He will give His people
    "Light at eventide."

In an hour of darkness,
    At the dead of night,
He will come,—and make us
    "Children of the Light."

Hail, thou sweet memorial
    Of the Saviour's birth!
Hail the hour that brought Him
    To our ruined earth!

We can face the darkness,
    His sure word our Light:
On His strong arm leaning,
    Ours no need for sight.

For His Advent waiting,
    We can suffer still;—
All is the fulfilling
    Of a loving will.

What is dark at present
    Shall one day be bright;
'Tis enough—the knowledge
    All GOD does is right.

We may toil in rowing
    On a storm-tossed sea,

'Mid Time's deepening darkness;—
He can steer,—and *see!*

He can lead us safely
To the viewless shore;
Every need supplying
From Love's boundless store.

We, His happy children,
Nothing have to fear;
What to *sight* is misty,
Is to *faith* all clear.

Hope in GOD our "Anchor";
Grateful love the spring
Of the streams of action,
Joyously we sing.

Pilgrims onward hastening
Through a land of Night,
To a "Home" *with* JESUS,
In a world of Light.

Another invalid whose quiet songs are borne to us upon the western wind, is Mary Shekleton, one of the many faithful *sofa* workers, who do what they can, and beyond that are "content to wait."

The following hymn, with its true deep longing, and yet restful confidence, will make Christian invalids feel that the writer is no stranger. As we read, a celestial chime blends with the pilgrim melody, and the promise rings out clear and full, "He will fulfil the desire of them that fear Him."

"THAT I MAY KNOW HIM."

One fervent wish, my God! it speaks the whole
And every longing of my weary soul;
To know my Saviour is my one desire—
The great high prize to which I most aspire.

To know Him in His depth of love to me,
The poorest, weakest, vilest though I be:
His lost one, whom He came to seek and save:
His loved one, for whose life Himself He gave.

To know Him as my chiefest, dearest Friend,
Who loveth, and will love me to the end;
Who feels my every pain, my griefs, my fears:
Who tasted oft the bitterness of tears.

To know Him as my wise and skilful Guide;
A pilgrim I, yet safe with Him beside;
The path to me untrodden heretofore,
He knoweth well, who traced each step before.

To know Him as the "All in all" to me:
All mine for time, all for eternity;
And in each gift of providence and grace,
Himself in all His loveliness to trace.

To know Him as He sits at God's right hand,
All things in heaven and earth at His command;
All, all are His, and what are His are mine;
Oh, what shall ever such rich grace outshine!

To know Him as earth's rightful King and Lord,
Who soon shall claim His great and full reward.
The travail of His soul He then shall see,
And at His feet creation bow the knee.

One other hymn by Mary Shekleton we must give. It points to the unfailing Source of all true "joy in tribulation," the contemplation of the love Divine "which passeth knowledge."

THE LOVE OF CHRIST.

It passeth knowledge, that dear love of Thine,
My Jesus, Saviour; yet this soul of mine
Would of Thy love, in all its breadth and length,
Its height, and depth, its everlasting strength,
             Know more and more.

It passeth telling, that dear love of Thine,
My Jesus, Saviour; yet these lips of mine

Would fain proclaim to sinners, far and near,
A love which can remove all guilty fear,
          And love beget.

It passeth praises, that dear love of Thine,
My Jesus, Saviour; yet this heart of mine
Would sing that love, so full, so rich, so free,
Which brings a rebel sinner, such as me,
          Nigh unto God.

But though I cannot sing, or tell, or know,
The fulness of Thy love while here below,
My empty vessel I may freely bring:
O Thou who art of love the living spring,
          My vessel fill!

I am an empty vessel—not one thought,
Or look of love, I ever to Thee brought;
Yet I may come, and come again to Thee,
With this, the empty sinner's only plea—
          Thou lovest me.

O fill me, Jesus, Saviour, with Thy love!
Lead, lead me to the living Fount above;
Thither may I, in simple faith draw nigh,
And never to another fountain fly,
          But unto Thee.

And when my Jesus face to face I see,
When at His lofty throne I bow the knee;
Then of His love, in all its breadth and length,
Its height and depth, its everlasting strength,
          My soul shall sing!

Our last " specimen," a very lovely and poetical one, we take from the hymns of Mrs. Crewdson, one of the few who combine exquisite elegance and imagination with deep and tender spirituality. She was an invalid for several years; but by this the Church of Christ was a gainer, as song after song was added to her " hymnal treasures." Her " little while " of suffering is past now, but its sweet results live on in such fair forms as the hymn we select.

"A LITTLE WHILE."

Oh! for the peace which floweth as a river,
   Making life's desert places bloom and smile:
Oh! for the faith to grasp heaven's bright "for ever."
   Amid the shadows of earth's "little while!"

"A little while" for patient vigil keeping,
   To face the stern, to wrestle with the strong;
"A little while," to sow the seed with weeping,
   Then bind the sheaves, and sing the harvest song.

"A little while" to wear the weeds of sadness,
   To pace with weary steps through miry ways;
Then to pour forth the fragrant oil of gladness,
   And clasp the girdle round the robe of praise.

"A little while," 'mid shadow and illusion,
   To strive, by faith, love's mysteries to spell;
Then read each dark enigma's bright solution:
   Then hail sight's verdict, He doeth all things well!"

"A little while," the earthen pitcher taking
   To wayside brooks, from far off fountains fed;
Then the cool lip its thirst for ever slaking
   Beside the fulness of the Fountain-head.

"A little while," to keep the oil from failing;
   "A little while," faith's flickering lamp to trim;
And then, the Bridegroom's coming footsteps hailing,
   To haste to meet Him with the bridal hymn.

And He who is Himself the Gift and Giver—
   The future glory and the present smile,
With the bright promise of the glad "for ever,"
   Will light the shadows of the "little while!"

Every verse is beautiful, but the last is probably amaranthine; I think it will live, suffering not by many a transplantation of quotation, when the acorns of to-day are the forest trees of another century.

IX.

SEVEN CLERICAL HYMN-WRITERS.

OUR Specimen-Glasses shall be filled in this chapter from a garden of rich variety, cultivation, and beauty. The selection of seven representative Hymn-writers among clergymen of the Church of England, and then of one or two representative hymns by each, has afforded more than common pleasure and satisfaction, mingled only with the regret that our Specimen Glasses cannot contain more.

The impression left on the mind by careful consideration of the large number of hymns from which this selection has been made is twofold.

First, the cultivated taste cannot fail to recognize in them a standard above the average. There is perfect refinement of expression; never a word that grates upon a sensitive ear; never a line that could be, fairly or unfairly, stigmatised as cant; rarely a verse which has not some impress of the "guinea stamp" in addition to the ring of the true "gowd."[1] It may be a homely way of putting it, but it is simple fact, that one instinctively feels every one of these hymns to be the work of a "gentleman," in the full sense of the word. And perhaps this characteristic can only be keenly appreciated by those who have waded through volumes of well-meaning hymns from other sources, which are devoid of this subtle essence of refinement, wincing, with what is almost pain, as the high and holy themes seem to be veiled or disfigured by an intangible tastelessness of style.

Secondly, a deeper pleasure is felt as we see how the Name which is above every name is peculiarly the keynote of all the sweet music of these consecrated singers. Among no other group of hymn-writers do we find quite so large a proportion of hymns distinctively and directly making melody unto or concerning the Lord Jesus Christ. Other groups have more of statement or meditation as to doctrines or experiences, but in this the personality of the beloved Lord is the central and overflowing fountain of song. "Jesus only" might be the motto of any collection containing hymns exclusively by Church of England clergymen. Not that in noting this we are undervaluing other groups, but it is cheering to find this sweet pre-eminence in praise of Him or to Him occupied by His ambassadors in our dear Church.

[1] gowd (a Scottish word): gold

Our first two specimens are by the Rev. S. J. Stone, author of " The Knight of Intercession, and other Poems," and of the well-known Thanksgiving Hymn for the recovery of the Prince of Wales, to which, however, our chosen " speci- mens" are unquestionably superior.

THE PENITENT.

Weary of earth and laden with my sin,
I look at heaven and long to enter in ;
But there no evil thing may find a home ;
And yet I hear a voice that bids me " Come."

So vile I am, how dare I hope to stand
In the pure glory of that holy land ?
Before the whiteness of that Throne appear ?
Yet there are hands stretched out to draw me near.

The while I fain would tread the heavenly way,
Evil is ever with me day by day ;
Yet on mine ears the gracious tidings fall—
" Repent, confess, thou shalt be loosed from all."

It is the voice of Jesus that I hear :
His are the hands stretch'd out to draw me near :
And His the blood that can for all atone,
And set me faultless there before the Throne.

'Twas He who found me on the deathly wild,
And made me heir of heaven, the Father's child :
And day by day, whereby my soul may live,
Gives me His grace of pardon, and will give.

O great Absolver, grant my soul may wear
The lowliest garb of penitence and prayer,
That in the Father's courts my glorious dress
May be the garment of Thy righteousness.

Yea, Thou wilt answer for me, Righteous Lord :
Thine all the merits, mine the great reward ;
Thine the sharp thorns, and mine the golden crown :
Mine the life won, and Thine the life laid down.

Nought can I bring, dear Lord, for all I owe:
Yet let my full heart what it can bestow;
Like Mary's gift, let my devotion prove,
Forgiven greatly, how I greatly love!

THE HARVEST OF SOULS.

Gather the Harvest in:
The fields are white, and long ago ye heard
Ringing across the world the Master's word—
    Leave not such fruitage to the lord of Sin:
    Gather the Harvest in.

Gather the Harvest in:
Souls dying and yet deathless, o'er the lands,
East, West, North, South, lie ready to your hands;
    Long since that other did his work begin;
    Gather the Harvest in.

Gather the Harvest in:
Rise early and reap late. Is this a time
For ease? Shall he, by every curse and crime,
    Out of your grasp the golden treasure win?
    Gather the Harvest in.

Gather the Harvest in:
Ye know ye live not to yourselves, nor die,
Then let not this bright hour of work go by:
    To all who know, and do not, there is sin:
    Gather the Harvest in.

Gather the Harvest in:
Soon shall the mighty Master summon home
For feast His reapers. Think ye they shall come
    Whose sickles gleam not, and whose sheaves are thin?
    Gather the Harvest in!

From these we pass to the most touching Confirmation Hymn extant, by
the Rev. John Ernest Bode, Rector of Castle Camps, near Cambridge. Oh that
this hymn could be, not only sung after every Confirmation, but learnt by every candidate, and fixed for life in memory and in heart! That first conscious

and voluntary act of Church membership, too often a mere rite, or an emotional day dream, would be what our Church intends it to be,—the entrance upon a life of consecration and privilege, of following fully, and serving joyously, if the spirit of this hymn were always that of the preparers and the prepared.

CONFIRMATION.

O Jesus! I have promised
  To serve Thee to the end;
Be Thou for ever near me,
  My Master and my Friend!
I shall not fear the battle
  If Thou art by my side,
Nor wander from the pathway
  If Thou wilt be my Guide.

Oh, let me feel Thee near me:
  The world is ever near;
I see the sights that dazzle,
  The tempting sounds I hear.
My foes are ever near me,
  Around me and within;
But Jesus, draw Thou nearer,
  And shield my soul from sin.

Oh let me hear Thee speaking,
  In accents clear and still,
Above the storms of passion,
  The murmurs of self-will.
Oh speak! to reassure me,
  To hasten or control;
Oh speak! to make me listen,
  Thou Guardian of my Soul.

Oh! let me see Thy features,
  The look that once could make
So many a true disciple
  Leave all things for Thy sake.
The look that beamed on Peter,
  When he Thy Name denied;

The look that draws Thy lovers
    Close to Thy piercèd side.

O Jesus! Thou hast promised
    To all who follow Thee,
That where Thou art in glory
    There shall Thy servant be;
And, Jesus, I have promised
    To serve Thee to the end;
Oh, give me grace to follow
    My Master and my Friend!

Oh, let me see Thy footmarks,
    And in them plant mine own;
My hope to follow duly
    Is in Thy strength alone.
Oh, guide me, call me, draw me,
    Uphold me to the end;
And then in heaven receive me,
    My Saviour and my Friend!

While, generally speaking, the instinct of adoring reverence would choose the title so often used by St. Paul, "the Lord Jesus," a yet deeper instinct, or rather insight, has in this case evidently suggested the simple use of the beloved Name alone. Here its very utterance seems strength-giving; and the reiteration of it in the fifth verse seems, not only to express, but to aid in the personal clinging to a personal Master and Saviour. It is not only in connection with a Confirmation season that the value of this hymn will be felt; but whenever the heart says,—

    "Lord, I my vows to Thee *renew*,"

it may follow as a shining seal upon that renewal, leaving each time a deeper and clearer impress.

The deeper and the oftener that seal is set, whether in spirit only, or in letter also, the readier shall we be to sing our next hymn, which needs no comment.

THE NAME OF JESUS.

There is a Name I love to hear:
    I love to sing its worth;

It sounds like music in mine ear,
　　The sweetest Name on earth.

It tells me of a Saviour's love,
　　Who died to set me free;
It tells me of His precious blood,
　　The sinner's perfect plea.

It tells me of a Father's smile
　　Beaming upon His child;
It cheers me through this little while,
　　Through desert, waste, and wild.

Jesus, the Name I love so well,
　　The Name I love to hear;
No saint on earth its worth can tell,
　　No heart conceive how dear.

This Name shall shed its fragrance still
　　Along this thorny road,
Shall sweetly smooth the rugged hill
　　That leads me up to God.

And there with all the blood-bought throng,
　　From sin and sorrow free,
I'll sing the new eternal song
　　Of Jesu's love to me!

This is by the Rev. Frederick Whitfield, whose hymn, "I need Thee, Precious Jesus," is too well known to call for quotation. There is a peculiar gentleness without weakness, and sweetness without sameness, in all his writings, which endear them greatly to all quiet-loving Christians.

A perfect little gem of fervent simplicity, deeply graven with the One Name in its sweet English form, is by the late Rev. John S. B. Monsell, L.L.D. Its first two lines soon become a permanent spirit-treasure. Again and again in weariness or worry, they come like a cool hand upon a burning brow:—

　　　　"To Thee, O dear, dear Saviour,
　　　　　My spirit turns for rest!'"

Perhaps the first line suggests,

　　　　"To thee, O dear, dear country,"

but its music is far sweeter, and its comfort far deeper. For one is perhaps very distant; the other is very near. There may be leagues of life yet to traverse before the "country" is reached, and the clearest telescope of faith can but give a glimpse of the "things not seen." But Jesus, the King of the far land of glory, the "dear, dear Saviour," is not far away. He is with us alway; for He hath said, "I will never leave thee."

JESUS PRECIOUS.

To Thee, O dear, dear Saviour,
   My spirit turns for rest;
My peace is in Thy favour,
   My pillow on Thy breast.

Though all the world deceive me,
   I know that I am Thine!
And Thou wilt never leave me,
   O blessèd Saviour mine:

O Thou whose mercy found me,
   From bondage set me free,
And then for ever bound me
   With threefold cords to Thee.

Oh for a heart to love Thee
   More truly as I ought,
And nothing place above Thee,
   In deed, or word, or thought!

Oh for that choicest blessing
   Of living in Thy love;
And thus on earth possessing
   The peace of heaven above!

This holy familiarity, this leaning upon the bosom of the beloved Saviour, so far from being incompatible with the deepest and lowliest reverence and awe, rather lead to it. The nearer we approach, and the more closely we cling to, the beloved Son of God, the more does He, in whom dwelleth all the fulness of the Godhead bodily, make known to us the Name of the Triune Jehovah with its infinite might and mystery, grace and glory.

Hence it is but what we may expect, when we find the same writer rising into a strain of concentrated and intense adoration of the "Undivided Trinity." The hymn we refer to is cast in the symbolic form of thrice tripled triplets, three divisions, each containing three stanzas of three lines,—a trinity of trinitarian trinities. The type of this form is found in Revelation 4:8.

THE TRINITY.

Mighty Father! Blessèd Son!
Holy Spirit! Three in One!
Evermore Thy will be done!

Threefold is Thy glorious might,
Threefold is Thy Name of light,
Holy! awful! infinite!

Threefold let our praises be,
Great mysterious One, to Thee!
Undivided Trinity!

Mystery of mysteries!
Before whom with veilèd eyes
Songs of saints and angels rise.

Rainbow-like the emerald zone
That encompasseth Thy Throne,
O Thou most mysterious One.

Thunderings and lightnings, rolled
From beneath, Thy saints enfold,
Clothed in white, and crowned with gold.

———

Holy, Holy, Holy, Lord!
God Almighty! Father! Word!
Spirit! Three in One adored!

Threefold is Thy love to me,
Threefold let my graces be—
Faith, and Hope, and Charity.

Mighty Father! Blessèd Son!
Holy Spirit! Three in One!
Evermore Thy will be done!

The name of the tune to this hymn—Havergal—No. *777* in "Songs of Grace and Glory," may excite remark; but it will not be wondered that this name was chosen, when we tell that it was the last ever written by that sainted hand which now bears one of the "harps of God"—written just before the Master's voice said "Come up higher." The tune with its serene melody and rich harmony is itself an epitome of his musical work.

Passing now to a writer whose exquisite touch reveals instead of disguising his spiritual themes,—the Rev. Godfrey Thring, Rector of Alford, Somerset,— the keynote of our group is again sounded, "Saviour, blessed Saviour!" The following remarkably beautiful hymn is very stimulating and inspiriting.

SONG OF THE PILGRIMAGE.

Saviour, blessèd Saviour,
　　Listen while we sing,
Hearts and voices raising
　　Praises to our King.
All we have to offer,
　　All we hope to be,—
Body, soul, and spirit:
　　All we yield to Thee.

Nearer, ever nearer,
　　Christ, we draw to Thee;
Deep in adoration
　　Bending low the knee;
Thou for our redemption
　　Camest on earth to die;
Thou, that we might follow,
　　Hast gone up on high.

Great and ever greater
　　Are Thy mercies here,
True and everlasting
　　Are the glories there;

Where no pain or sorrow,
    Toil or care, is known,
Where the angel legions
    Circle round Thy Throne.

Dark and ever darker
    Was the wintry past,
Now a ray of gladness
    O'er our path is cast;
Every day that passeth,
    Every hour that flies,
Tells of love unfeignèd,
    Love that never dies.

Clearer still and clearer
    Dawns the light from heaven,
In our sadness bringing
    News of sin forgiven;
Life has lost its shadows,
    Pure the light within;
Thou hast shed Thy radiance
    On a world of sin.

Brighter still and brighter
    Glows the western sun,
Shedding all its gladness
    O'er our work that's done;
Time will soon be over;
    Toil and sorrow past:
May we, blessèd Saviour,
    Find a rest at last.

Onward, ever onward,
    Journeying o'er the road
Worn by saints before us,
    Journeying on to God,
Leaving all behind us,
    May we hasten on,
Backward never looking
    Till the prize is won.

> Bliss, all bliss excelling,
>   When the ransomed soul
> Earthly toils forgetting
>   Finds its promised goal;
> Where in joys unheard of
>   Saints with angels sing,
> Never weary raising
>   Praises to their King. Amen.

Still the song is "Jesus only," as we turn to another hymn by the same writer, to whom more than almost any other we look for really valuable additions to our Church of England hymnological treasures.

THE ADVENT.

Jesus came (the heavens adoring), came with peace from realms on high;
Jesus came for man's redemption, lowly came on earth to die.
Hallelujah, Hallelujah! came in deep humility.

Jesus comes again in mercy, when our hearts are bowed with care;
Jesus comes again in answer to our earnest heartfelt prayer.
Hallelujah, Hallelujah! Comes to save us from despair.

Jesus comes to hearts rejoicing, bringing news of sin forgiven;
Jesus comes in sounds of gladness, leading souls redeemed to heaven.
Hallelujah, Hallelujah! Now the gate of death is riven.

Jesus comes in joy and sorrow, shares alike our hopes and fears;
Jesus comes, whate'er befalls us, glads our hearts and dries our tears.
Hallelujah, Hallelujah! Cheering e'en our failing years.

Jesus comes on clouds triumphant, when the heavens shall pass away;
Jesus comes again in glory,—let us then our homage pay!
Hallelujah! ever singing, till the dawning of the day.

The last verse leads us onward to "that blessed hope, and the glorious appearing of the great God and our Saviour Jesus Christ." Yet we "who love His appearing," may perhaps dwell too little on the solemnities of His "coming again with glory to judge both the quick and the dead." And as in our Prayer-Book, so in our Church of England Hymns, we find "a rightly dividing" and a wise proportioning of the Word of Truth. One aspect we find in the solemn grandeur of a hymn by the Rev. J. A. Latrobe, Honorary Canon of Carlisle.

THE ADVENT.

Day of vengeance! loud resounding,
　　Hark! the thrilling trumpet's swell,
Peal on peal o'er earth rebounding,
　　Nature's universal knell;
　　　　Deeply echoing,
　　Bursts the bands of death and hell.

O'er the ruins of creation
　　See on high the Crucified,
'Mid the widening devastation,
　　On the wings of whirlwinds ride.
　　　　Man before Him
　　Bows the spirit of His pride.

Lo! the dead in thronging numbers,
　　Awestruck at His stern command,
Springing from their iron slumbers,
　　Round the dread tribunal stand,
　　　　View with trembling
　　Judgment in His red right hand.

O Immanuel! spirit-broken,
　　At Thy piercèd feet I lie;
What my hope? Behold that token!
　　See that blood-stained Cross on high.
　　　　Glorious symbol,
　　Brightly beaming on my eye.

By Thy griefs on wild or mountain,
　　By Thine agonizing groan,
By Thy life-spring's purple fountain,
　　By Thy dark sepulchral stone,—
　　　　O Immanuel,
　　Save me, prostrate at Thy throne.

The other aspect comes out in the thrilling Communion Hymn by the Rev. E. H. Bickersteth. Very simple, but almost unaccountably touching is this little hymn, so full of hidden power. But it is from the pen of our first living Christian poet, who would have been the idol of the literary world if he had spent the very same amount of thought and power and art and beauty upon secular or even semi-sacred themes as he has displayed in his great poem, "Yesterday, To-day, and For ever," of which "Till He come" is a tiny but melodious echo. "*Only* 'till He come'"! But what an *only!* Well may we "with patience wait" through the "little while."

"TILL HE COME."

Till He come! Oh let the words
Linger on the trembling chords!
Let the little while between
In their golden light be seen;
Let us think how heaven and home
Lie beyond that "Till He come."

When the weary ones we love
Enter on their rest above,
Seems the earth so poor and vast,
All our life-joy overcast?
Hush! be every murmur dumb,—
It is only "Till He come."

Clouds and conflicts round us press;
Would we have one sorrow less?
All the sharpness of the cross,
All that tells the world is loss,
Death, and darkness, and the tomb,
Only whisper "Till He come."

See the feast of love is spread:
Drink the wine, and break the bread,—
Sweet memorials,—till the Lord
Calls us round His heavenly board;
Some from earth, from glory some,
Severed only "Till He come."

X.

MISSION HYMNS.

PERHAPS no movement in the Church of England is or ever has been more remarkable than the "Mission Week" movement. In this work hymn-singing has borne no unimportant part. Since the days of the Reformation, when Luther's grand Evangelical Chorales were one of the most powerful means of spreading the truth of God till all Germany resounded with the music of the "good tidings," there has been perhaps nothing to compare with the similar influence of holy song during the last year or two. Specimens of "Hymns by Recent or Less-known Writers" would be very incompletely selected without a few pages devoted to those which have been and are continually being used and owned by our God in this special work of ingathering, this very harvest of souls which He is giving to our beloved Church of England.

Not so very long ago there was a pretty general impression that the best plan was to use only very well-known and old-established favourites at Mission Services, and that this was the only way to secure hearty singing and to make any useful impression by it. When "Songs of Grace and Glory for Mission Services" was first projected, a friend remarked:—"Then of course you will take care that it contains only the old favourites, which every one knows and every one can sing!" Oh, the blessing which would have been missed had this counsel been followed, and had "*only* the old favourites" been admitted!

The practical working of it is this: We want a Mission Week to be everywhere, as one pastor testified that it had been, among his own flock, "the beginning of a new era"; we want it to startle and arouse; to set people thinking; to show them that the old life of carelessness, or the old ruts and grooves of half-hearted service will not do; that there is more to be had and more to be done, and that to-day must not be as yesterday. Now if, at such times, only such hymns and tunes are sung as people have been familiar with all their lives, one great means of this arousing is sacrificed. Such hymns and tunes, even if intrinsically superior to the new ones (which is by no means to be taken for granted), slip far too easily through the mind and off the tongue. The careless are not often arrested by what they have sung fifty times before. The believer may be solaced and soothed by some "dear old hymn," but he is not roused by it to see that even for him there is newness of life to be sought, new fruit unto holiness to be brought forth. All classes can sing "Come, let us join our cheerful songs," or "How sweet the Name of Jesus sounds" with plenty of vocal effect and pleasant warmth and enjoyment, but without being probed and stirred on the one hand, or lifted as on eagle wings into glorious liberty and glowing consecration on the other. But when new hymns are used, attention is caught, striking expressions are infixed, the old groove is broken through, and thus a way opened for yet further stirring; the hymn-book is recurred to because some haunting line "rings in the ears" as we say, but more truly "rings in the heart." Rings perhaps as the knell of all hope in self-righteousness and effort; rings perhaps as the first echo in the soul of the joyful sound of the Gospel; rings perhaps as an answering chime to the "bells of the City," the nearing of heaven's own music.

The influence thus exercised will be found to be not evanescent, but enduring. Hymns which were sung during the solemn and blessed "Mission-Week" will always be a key to its holy memories, or rather an electric wire rekindling, with instantaneous flash the brightness and fervour of those wonderful hours when "Jesus of Nazareth" was felt to be "passing by."

Not long ago a few casual chords were played on an organ, only to try the stops, and they glided, perhaps were *guided*, into the tune "Zaanaim," which was repeated with another combination of stops. At the first pause the bellows-blower came round to the player, evidently under strong emotion, and with tears in his eyes. "Please to excuse me," he said, "but oh, that was 'Take Salvation'!" This unexpected interruption naturally led to a conversation. The tune had recalled the refrain of the hymn, and that had brought up vividly all the impressions of a very blessed Mission Week held in the place some months before. We give it as being one of those hymns which have been found peculiarly useful, both in arresting and winning souls, and also in reviving and fixing impressions previously made.

"TAKE SALVATION."

Hark! the voice of Jesus calling,
    "Come, thou laden, come to Me;
I have rest and peace to offer;
    Rest, poor labouring one, for thee;
        Take salvation,
        Take it now, and happy be."

Yes, though high in heavenly glory,
    Still the Saviour calls to thee;

Faith can hear His gracious accents—
"Come, thou laden, come to Me;
Take salvation,
Take it now, and happy be."

Soon that Voice will cease its calling,
Now it speaks, and speaks to thee;
Sinner, heed the gracious message,
To the blood for refuge flee;
Take salvation,
Take it now, and happy be.

Life is found alone in Jesus,
Only there 'tis offered thee—
Offered without price or money,
'Tis the gift of God sent free;
Take salvation,
Take it now, and happy be!

Albert Midlane, 1865.

It has been found that, generally speaking, the success of a Mission Week has borne a very marked proportion to the previous preparation. Suddenly or hurriedly undertaken, there has rarely been a full blessing. But where for weeks or even months there has been fervent supplication, a "continuing in prayer" with faith, and much "agreeing together," there, as a rule, the blessing has been rich and abundant. But it is easy to see how this "spirit of grace and of supplication" may be instrumentally awakened and quickened and fostered, if, instead of letting the choir and congregation go on in the old routine of the usual hymns, such as the following are sung week after week. They awaken interest or at least queries from outsiders, and give stimulus to prayer and reality to expectation among "the Lord's remembrancers."

I shall never forget the thrilling effect of a hymn sung in a country church two months before a Mission Week. The sermon was very fervent and faithful, dwelling on the promise of "showers of blessing" (Ezekiel 34:26), and inviting the hearers to seek and claim its gracious fulfilment among themselves. At the close, breaking the usual routine of concluding the morning service with prayer only, the preacher gave out this little hymn, somewhat to the surprise of many. But the strange intensity of fervour with which it was sung showed that it was the truest sealing of the preacher's words, and I know that it bore much fruit of faith and prayer.

" SHOWERS OF BLESSING."

"Showers of blessing!" gracious promise,
    From the God who rules on high:
From the everlasting Father,
    He who will not, cannot lie:
      Showers of blessing
    He has promised from the sky.

"Showers of blessing!" joyful showers,
    Making every heart rejoice:
Come, ye saints, and plead the promise,
    Raise in faith the suppliant voice;
      Showers of blessing,
    Oh! let nothing less suffice!

Albert Midlane, 1865.

The next hymns have also been found most useful in thus "going before the Face of the Lord to prepare His ways."

TIMES OF REFRESHING.

Father, for Thy promised blessing
    Still we plead before Thy throne;
For the times of sweet refreshing,
    Which can come from Thee alone.

Blessèd earnests Thou hast given,
    But in these we would not rest;
Blessings still with Thee are hidden:
    Pour them forth, and make us blest.

Prayer ascendeth to Thee ever:
    Answer! Father, answer prayer;
Bless, oh, bless each weak endeavour,
    Blood-bought pardon to declare!

Wake Thy slumbering children, wake them,
    Bid them to Thy harvest go:
Blessings, O our Father, make them:
    Round their steps let blessings flow.

Give reviving, give refreshing,
    Give the looked-for jubilee;
To Thyself may crowds be pressing,
    Bringing glory unto Thee.

Let no hamlet be forgotten,
    Let Thy showers on all descend;
That in one loud blessèd anthem
    Myriads may in triumph blend!

Albert Midlane, 1865.

" REVIVE THY WORK."

Revive Thy work, O Lord,
    Thy mighty arm make bare;
Speak with the voice that wakes the dead,
    And make Thy people hear.

Revive Thy work, O Lord,
    Disturb this sleep of death;
Quicken the smouldering embers now
    By Thine Almighty breath.

Revive Thy work, O Lord,
    Create soul-thirst for Thee;
And hungering for the bread of life,
    Oh may our spirits be!

Revive Thy work, O Lord,
    Exalt Thy precious Name;
And, by the Holy Ghost, our love
    For Thee and Thine inflame.

Revive Thy work, O Lord,
    And give refreshing showers;
The glory shall be all Thine own,
    The blessing, Lord, be ours!

Albert Midlane, 1865.

For preliminary prayer meetings of workers, what can be more touching than the following?

"CALL THEM IN."

"Call them in!" the poor, the wretched,
　　Sin-stained wanderers from the fold;
Peace and pardon freely offer,—
　　Can you weigh their worth with gold?
"Call them in!"—the weak, the weary,
　　Laden with the doom of sin;
Bid them come and rest in Jesus,
　　He is waiting;—"call them in!"

"Call them in!"—the Jew, the Gentile;
　　Bid the stranger to the feast;
"Call them in!"—the rich, the noble,
　　From the highest to the least.
Forth the Father runs to meet them,
　　He hath all their sorrows seen;
Robe and ring and royal sandals
　　Wait the lost ones;—"call them in!"

"Call them in!"—the broken-hearted,
　　Cowering 'neath the brand of shame;
Speak love's message, low and tender,—
　　"'Twas for sinners Jesus came."
See! the shadows lengthen round us,
　　Soon the day-dawn will begin;
Can you leave them lost and lonely?
　　Christ is coming;—"call them in!"

Anna Shipton, circa 1868.

Oh that even reading this hymn on this page may be the means of calling forth a true "Here am I, send me!" from some Christian lips, which have hitherto been slow to speak for Jesus and to try to tell of His salvation and of His love! And oh that many more may be made willing not only to "call" "the poor, the wretched," but bravely, wisely, and lovingly as the Master may give opportunity, to "call in" "the *rich, the noble!*" Oh the aching hearts under silk and velvet! Oh the weary hands filled with silver and gold! Oh the "empty void" under the surface of glittering life! How one longs for these to be called to the feast! these, who might in their turn call so many others, if only they had heard the voice of the King for themselves.

But we have digressed. It is most useful to have open practises, or "hymn-meetings," for some time before a Mission Week. Some will come to these who will not come to the preliminary prayer-meetings. The spiritual end and aim of such practisings should be very prominent. They afford an excellent opportunity for reaching persons not otherwise easily reached, and awakening and fostering interest in the whole subject, as well as being direct preparation for the services. Especially if the attendance is very large, and many are singing by ear, much time is saved by the simple plan of learning the tunes *line by line,* each line being separately learnt by heart. It may seem childish till tried, but it is always liked and always effectual. A tune worked at in this way, brisk and bright, for six or seven minutes, is sung more accurately, and with more "swing" and certainty, than would be attained by twenty minutes of "singing it straight through." After this, true and beautiful musical expression is *best* attained by pointing out the *truths* which we are singing. For instance, in this verse—no direction of, "Third line crescendo!" would produce so good and musical effect as a few bright happy words calling attention to Christ being indeed "my peace, my *strength,* my JOY, my CROWN!"

A most useful little hymn for opening either the Mission Week, or any single service, is the following. Perhaps no other expresses in such short compass so exactly what we want at such a season. Every line is telling. It is a twelve-line epitome of Mission Week desires and work.

"O HOLY SPIRIT, COME!"

> O Holy Spirit, come,
> And Jesu's love declare;
> Oh tell us of our heavenly home,
> And guide us safely there.
>
> Our unbelief remove,
> By Thy almighty breath:
> Oh work the wondrous work of love,
> The mighty work of faith.
>
> Come with resistless power,
> Come with almighty grace,
> Come with the long expected shower,
> And fall upon this place.

Oswald Allen, 1862.

XI.

MISSION HYMNS—*(Continued).*

PERHAPS in mission work no hymn has been more used and blessed than "Lord, I hear of showers of blessing," * by the able and devoted Editor of *Woman's Work;* but it is too well known for quotation here. So also is another, equally familiar, "There is life for a look at the Crucified One," by Amelia Matilda Hull, which has been God's message of peace to many an anxious one. But the three following hymns are less known, and yet have been greatly blessed. The first has a touching beauty of expression which makes it especially suitable for Mission Services in an educated congregation.

"COME UNTO ME."

"Come unto Me, ye weary,
    And I will give you Rest."
O blessèd voice of JESUS,
    Which comes to hearts opprest;
It tells of benediction,
    Of pardon, grace, and peace:
Of joy that hath no ending,
    Of love which cannot cease.

"Come unto Me, ye wanderers,
    And I will give you Light."
O loving voice of JESUS,
    Which comes to cheer the night;
Our hearts were filled with sadness,
    And we had lost our way;

* The tune "Persis," No. 187 in Havergal's Psalmody, forms the most touching and beautiful accompaniment to this hymn, and, though new, is already a favourite. Hymn 120, "Hear the Father's ancient promise," is very precious, and with the above tune, Persis, is greatly prized. So likewise Hymn 191, "O Saviour, precious Saviour" (to the tune Zoan I.), the refrain of which, varying slightly in each verse, brings out a grand and solemn burst of praise. Both these hymns, 120 and 191, are deservedly great favourites.

But He has brought us gladness
And songs at break of day.

"Come Unto Me, ye fainting,
And I will give you Life."
O cheering voice of JESUS,
Which comes to aid our strife;
The foe is stern and eager,
The fight is fierce and long;
But He has made us mighty,
And stronger than the strong.

"And whosoever cometh,
I will not cast him out."
O welcome voice of JESUS,
Which drives away our doubt;
Which calls us, very sinners,
Unworthy though we be
Of love so free and boundless,
To come, dear LORD, to Thee.

William Chatterton Dix, 1867.

Yet I have seen even more hearts moved by the simple "Come, and Welcome," with its more homely phraseology, just as with "Take salvation," quoted above.

"COME, AND WELCOME."

Come, and welcome, to the Saviour,
He in mercy bids thee come;
Come, be happy in His favour,
Longer from Him do not roam;
Come, and welcome:
Come to Jesus, sinner, come!

Come, and welcome; rise to glory,
Leave this passing world behind:
Christ will spread His banner o'er Thee,
Thou in Him a Friend shalt find;

Come, and welcome,
To a Saviour good and kind.

Come, and welcome: do not linger,
　Make thy happy choice to-day;
True thou art a guilty sinner,
　But He'll wash thy sins away:
　　Come, and welcome,
　Time admits of no delay!

Albert Midlane, 1865.

These sweet invitations are, however, not all that is needed. Distinct expressions of simple faith and trust are most useful in lifting anxious ones out of the miry clay of doubt, and setting their feet upon the Rock, and putting a new song in their mouths. Many a trembling foot has found the following hymn a stepping-stone into "peace and joy in believing." For use during after-meetings, those happy times of drawing the nets, and often of astonishment at the draught, it has been found to be not only peculiarly suitable, but peculiarly blessed. Hearts which have dared to whisper for the first time, "Jesus, I will trust Thee," have been led on during the singing of this hymn, by the Spirit's power, to the song of happy faith, "Jesus, I *do* trust Thee, trust without a doubt!"

TRUST IN JESUS.

Jesus, I will trust Thee, trust Thee with my soul;
Guilty, lost, and helpless, Thou canst make me whole.
There is none in heaven or on earth like Thee:
Thou hast died for sinners—therefore, Lord, for me.

Jesus, I may trust Thee, Name of matchless worth
Spoken by the angel at Thy wondrous birth;
Written, and for ever, on Thy cross of shame,
Sinners read and worship, trusting in that Name.

Jesus, I must trust Thee, pondering Thy ways,
Full of love and mercy all Thine earthly days:
Sinners gathered round Thee, lepers sought Thy Face—
None too vile or loathsome for a Saviour's grace.

Jesus, I can trust Thee, trust Thy written Word,
Though Thy voice of pity I have never heard.
When Thy Spirit teacheth, to my taste how sweet—
Only may I hearken, sitting at Thy feet.

Jesus, I do trust Thee, trust without a doubt:
"Whosoever cometh, Thou wilt not cast out";
Faithful is Thy promise, precious is Thy blood;
These my soul's salvation, Thou my Saviour God!"[1]

Towards the close of a Mission Week, conducted in prayer and faith, and in the power of the Spirit of God, there is sure to be a spirit of praise and joy. And this, not because of the growing delight and zeal in the work, or because we are glad of the success of our efforts, nor even because of the great joy of seeing souls brought to the Lord Jesus; but because old and new believers alike, if the power of the Spirit is indeed among us, find Jesus Himself to be so very present and so very precious. And while the converts in the fervour of their new love and happiness in Him delight in and are strengthened by its expression in the most joyous hymns, I appeal to any who have been privileged to be fellow-workers in this most happy work, whether they do not also crave some bright new outpouring of their love to the Master and joy in Himself. And the same joyful hymns sometimes stir mightily those who are still "lingering just outside" to come and touch the hem of that loving Saviour's garment who has made others so very glad.

As perhaps pre-eminently suitable for this we would mention "I've *found* the Pearl of greatest price!" Oh, the exquisite delight of singing this most jubilant and suggestive little hymn at such a time, knowing that it is the very heart-song of many around. Two centuries old, and yet it always seems a new song! It is so full of Christ;—not one bit of self, except the appropriating "*My*," upon which indeed all its brightness hinges, for what is "*a* Christ" to us till we can say "*My* Christ!" *Then* He is "All in all!" I do not think any one who loves Jesus could ever be tired of singing this hymn.

"CHRIST ALL AND IN ALL."

I've found the Pearl of greatest price,
My heart doth sing for joy;

---

[1] This hymn was written by Mary Jane (Deck) Walker (1816–1878). F.R.H. sang the first verse, set to her hymntune "Hermas," faintly but clearly, ten minutes before her death June 3, 1879. See page 377 of Volume IV of the Havergal edition.

And sing I must, a Christ I have—
Oh what a Christ have I!

Christ is a Prophet, Priest, and King;
A Prophet full of light,
A Priest that stands 'twixt God and man,
A King that rules with might.

My Christ, He is the Lord of lords,
He is the King of kings;
He is the Sun of Righteousness,
With healing in His wings.

My Christ, He is the Tree of Life,
Who in God's garden grows,
Whose fruit does feed, whose leaves do heal;
My Christ is Sharon's Rose.

Christ is my meat, Christ is my drink,
My medicine and my health;
My peace, my strength, my joy, my crown,
My glory and my wealth.

Christ is my father and my friend,
My brother and my love;
My head, my hope, my Counsellor,
My Advocate above.

My Christ, He is the heaven of heavens,
My Christ, what shall I call!
My Christ is first, my Christ is last,
My Christ is All in All!

John Mason, 1683.

So far from any resting in present attainments, or, still worse, deliberately expecting reaction and coolness and failure, as too many do, we shall find that the *true* results of such times of special seeking and receiving blessing, both as to congregations and individuals, will be continuance and progress. The grace then given will be used and traded with, so that more may be given—" grace for

grace"; there will be more "reaching forward unto those things which are before," more pressing "toward the mark"; and the very tests and temptations and
trials which may follow the "times of refreshing" will only prove the reality of
the blessing. Thus the inspiriting pilgrim song, "Onward, upward, homeward!"
is peculiarly helpful and suitable for the close of a Mission Week.

"ONWARD, UPWARD, HOMEWARD!"

"Onward, upward, homeward!" hastily I flee,
From this world of sorrow, with my Lord to be;
Onward to the glory, upward to the prize,
Homeward to the mansions far above the skies.

"Onward, upward, homeward!" Here I find no rest;
Treading o'er the desert which my Saviour pressed;
"Onward, upward, homeward!" I shall soon be there,
Soon its joys and pleasures, I, through grace, shall share.

"Onward, upward, homeward!" Come along with me:
Ye who love the Saviour, bear me company;
"Onward, upward, homeward!" press with vigour on,
Yet a little moment, and the race is won!

Albert Midlane, 1864.

Note: This is the end of Rev. Bullock's posthumously published volume of
F.R.H.'s essays on hymns, concluding with the hymn by Albert Midlane.

The next three "Specimen-Glasses" were published in other books: F.R.H.'s
last, unfinished Specimen-Glass on hymns by Horatius Bonar, and her sister
Miriam's Specimen-Glass on hymns by F.R.H., were published in *Footprints and
Living Songs*, a prose volume of pieces by and about F.R.H. (London: Home
Words Publishing Office, 1883? date uncertain). Miriam's Specimen-Glass on
hymns by William Henry Havergal was published as Chapter 7 in her biography
Records of the Life of the Rev. William Henry Havergal, M.A. (London: Home
Words Publishing Office, 1882).

H. Bonar.   "He has come."   J. Dürrner.

He has come, the Christ of God,
Left for us His glad abode,
Stooping from His throne of bliss
To this darksome wilderness.

He has come, the Prince of Peace;
Come to bid our sorrows cease;
Come to scatter with His light
All the shadows of our night.

He, the Mighty King, has come,
Making this poor earth His home;
Come to bear our sin's sad load,
Son of David, Son of God.

He has come, whose name of grace
Speaks deliverance to our race;
Left for us His glad abode,
Son of Mary, Son of God.

Unto us a son is given,
He has come from God's own heaven,
Bringing with Him from above
Holy peace and holy love.

This copy of a hymn by Bonar was written in F.R.H.'s hand, found in a hand-written Album of texts without the music. J. Dürrner was the composer of the music for this hymn. This likely was the German composer Johannes Ruprecht Julius Dürrner (1810–1859). Dürrner lived for a number of years in Edinburgh, where he taught music, and very possibly he knew Horatius Bonar.

Horatius Bonar (1808–1889).

HYMNS OF THE REV. HORATIUS BONAR, D.D.

BY THE LATE FRANCES RIDLEY HAVERGAL.

PROBABLY not one of our "recent" hymn-writers is so "well known" as Dr. Bonar; certainly no poet of the sanctuary has a firmer hold upon South as well as North as a loved and recognised leader in hymns of Faith and Hope. While we may find individual hymns here and there which reach the same high level of true human heart-melody with Divine harmony, we do not find many writers pouring out such copious streams from the "fountain of their singing." So that to him has been given the double privilege of contributing largely to the Hymnal treasures of the Church of Christ, and also of enriching her with more than one of those imperishable gems, deeply graven with truth, beauty, and power, which seal their impress upon the hearts and memories of all her members, and will be heirlooms of the family of God until earthly generations have passed away for ever.

These need no quotation: we all know them by heart; almost every line has taken rank among our spiritual household words. It is rather remarkable that those which appear to have reached this high position are chiefly, if not all, in the first person singular, and testify directly and personally of the Lord's dealings with the soul and the soul's respondings to Him. This personality is reality; and reality, whether in poetry or in spiritual life, is always power. It is what a writer really feels or has felt, and not what he supposes others to feel, which comes home. For "as in water face answereth to face, so the heart of man to man." Not "men to men"!

Some high authorities have strongly advocated the exclusion of the singular, and the use of the plural only, in hymns for "the great congregation." But "the sweet Psalmist of Israel" was not thus minded, by far the larger number of his inspired songs being in the first person singular. What a force and glow there is in his personal praise: "*I* love the Lord:" "*I* will sing:" "While *I* live will *I* praise the Lord." What pathetic power in his personal pleading: "Have mercy upon *me*:" "hear *me*:" "look upon *me*." What felt reality in "*my* soul thirsteth for Thee:" "*my* heart is fixed." What aid to appropriating faith in "The Lord is *my* Shepherd, *my* Rock, *my* Fortress, and *my* Deliverer; *my* God, *my* Strength."

It would be a bold paraphrase which dared the loss of pluralizing all these!

We "believe" in and rejoice in "the communion of saints," and know the power of song when "the singers were as one to make one sound to be heard in praising and thanking the Lord;" but this is rather enhanced than diminished when the whole force of individuality is thrown into each voice, and the energy and reality of the "I" is only multiplied and not merged in the "We."

Perhaps the four most widely known and valued hymns by Dr. Bonar are, "I heard the voice of Jesus say"—sweetest of all with its winning testimony to His realized grace and love; "I lay my sins on Jesus"—on whom, indeed, Jehovah has already laid them; "I was a wandering sheep"—an exquisite story of tender mercy and lovingkindness; and, "Thy way, not mine, O Lord." But we pass to some less familiar.

One of the happiest, brightest hymns we know is the following:—

"JESUS, SUN AND SHIELD ART THOU."

Jesus, Sun and Shield art Thou,
    Sun and Shield for ever!
Never canst Thou cease to shine,
    Cease to guard us, never.
Cheer our steps as on we go:
Come between us and the foe.

Jesus, Bread and Wine art Thou,
    Wine and Bread for ever!
Never canst Thou cease to feed
    Or refresh us, never.
Feed we still on bread Divine,
Drink we still this heavenly wine.

Jesus, Love and Life art Thou,
    Life and Love for ever!
Ne'er to quicken shalt Thou cease,
    Or to love us, never.
All of life and love we need
Is in Thee, in Thee indeed.

Jesus, Peace and Joy art Thou,
    Joy and Peace for ever!
Joy that fades not, changes not,
    Peace that leaves us never.

Joy and peace we have in Thee,
Now and through eternity.

Jesus, Song and Strength art Thou,
    Strength and Song for ever!
Strength that never can decay,
    Song that ceaseth never.
Still to us this strength and song
Through eternal days prolong!

There is great weakness in vain repetition: there is great strength in judicious and telling reiteration of thoughts which are in themselves inexhaustible. A skillfully wrought musical theme in a chorus or symphony recurs again and again and again, each time taking deeper hold upon the ear and feelings, appearing more striking and beautiful, and giving greater delight at each recurrence. So in the singing of this hymn (I do not say in a mere glancing through) the "Ever" and the "Never" of the first verse might be easily passed over, though indeed they are all-inclusive; but they come again, emphasized by the illustrating chords of the sweet old tune *Minden,* and our attention is fixed on them; they come again and again, and by the end of the hymn they are sealed on the memory, and often, very often, on the heart too. Again, there is a threefold repetition of the thought of Jesus which each verse sets forth, and this is very sweet and very gladdening to the loving heart which delights to linger on each gracious aspect of its precious Lord.

We pass to one or two of Dr. Bonar's experimental hymns. They take us by the hand, as it were, lifting us to a higher level of happy experience. Such expressions of confidence seem to be often blessed to the souls of other "children of the King" who may have "gone mourning." They excite desire for the same blessed assurance, and arouse faith and expectation from "the same Lord" who is "rich unto all that call upon Him." Perhaps such hymns are one form of that *"communication of faith,"* which *"may become effectual by the acknowledging of every good thing which is in you in Christ Jesus"* (Philemon 6).

"YES, FOR ME, FOR ME HE CARETH."

Yes, for me, for me He careth
    With a brother's tender care;
Yes, with me, with me He shareth
    Every burden, every fear.

Yes, o'er me, o'er me He watcheth—
    Ceaseless watcheth, night and day
Yes, e'en me, e'en me He snatcheth
    From the perils of the way.

Yes, for me He standeth pleading
    At the mercy-seat above;
Ever for me interceding,
    Constant in untiring love.

Yes, in me abroad He sheddeth
    Joys unearthly—love and light;
And to cover me He spreadeth
    His paternal wing of might.

Yes, in me, in me He dwelleth—
    I in Him, and He in me!
And my empty soul He filleth
    Here and through eternity.

Thus I wait for His returning,
    Singing all the way to heaven;
Such the joyful song of morning,
    Such the tranquil song of even!

The following is another beautiful and most encouraging hymn:—

"BE STILL, MY SOUL."

Be still, my soul, Jehovah loveth thee!
    Fret not, nor murmur at thy weary lot;
Though dark and lone thy journey seems to be,
    Be sure that thou art ne'er by Him forgot.
He ever loves; then trust Him, trust Him still:
Let all thy care be this—the doing of His will.

Thy hand in His, like fondest, happiest child,
    Place thou, nor draw it for a moment thence;
Walk thou with Him, a Father reconciled,
    Till in His own good time He calls thee hence.

Walk with Him now; so shall thy way be bright,
And all thy soul be filled with His most glorious light.

Take courage, faint not, though the foe be strong,
    Christ is thy strength! He fighteth on thy side:
Swift be thy race; remember, 'tis not long,
    The goal is near; the prize He will provide:
And then from earthly toil thou restest ever;
Never again to toil, or fight, or fear—oh! never.

He comes with His reward: 'tis just at hand;
    He comes in glory to His promised throne.
My soul, rejoice! ere long thy feet shall stand
    Within the city of the Blessèd One.
Thy perils past, thy heritage secure,
Thy tears all wiped away, thy joy for ever sure!

There is a wonderful *hush* in the first line of this hymn. It is like a great hand, very tender, very loving, and very strong, firmly laid upon a fluttering heart; one of those lines which, once felt and appropriated, are our own for ever, never losing their first power.

The well-known hymn beginning—

    All that I was, my sin, my guilt,
        My death, was all my own:
    All that I am I owe to Thee,
        My gracious God, alone—

is a short, clear, and pithy hymn of contrasted experience. But the hymn beginning, "I thought upon my sins," cast in the same antithetical form, is more personal and more touching still.

"I THOUGHT UPON MY SINS."

I thought upon my sins, and I was sad,
    My soul was troubled sore, and filled with pain;
But then I thought on Jesus, and was glad;
    My heavy grief was turned to joy again.

I thought upon the law, the fiery law—
    Holy, and just, and good in its decree;
I looked to Jesus, and in Him I saw
    That law fulfilled, its curse endured for me.

I thought I saw an angry, frowning God,
    Sitting as Judge upon the great white throne;
My soul was overwhelmed; then Jesus showed
    His gracious face, and all my dread was gone.

I saw my sad estate, condemned to die;
    Then terror seized upon my heart, and dark despair;
But when to Calvary I turned my eye,
    I saw the cross, and read forgiveness there.

I saw that I was lost, far gone astray,
    No hope of safe return there seemed to be;
But then I heard that Jesus was the Way,
    A new and living Way prepared for me.

Then in that Way—so free, so safe, so sure—
    Sprinkled all o'er with reconciling blood,
Will I abide, and never wander more,
    Walking along in fellowship with God!

Passing from the instances of Dr. Bonar's gift as a writer of experimental hymns, we must glance at another group in which he also excels—the spurring and stimulating appeals to "press toward the mark," or to "go work in the Master's vineyard."

OH, 'TIS NOT WHAT WE FANCIED IT.

Oh, 'tis not what we fancied it—
    This world, this world of ours;
We thought its skies were sunshine all,
    And all its fields were flowers.

But soon o'erclouded are its skies,
    Its flowers they fade away;
Our youthful hopes are vanishing,
    Our early joys decay.

Another light is breaking bright,
    Which beams from heaven on high;
And other flowers are blossoming,
    Which cannot fade or die.

Above us is a brighter land,
    To which we seek to come;
Our sure and quiet resting-place,
    Our everlasting home.

Its fields are ever beautiful,
    Its skies are ever fair,
Its day is always clear and bright,
    For Christ, its Sun, is there.

O Sun of Righteousness, arise,
    Thy light upon us beam;
For all this life is but a sleep,
    And all this world a dream!

MAKE HASTE, O MAN, TO LIVE!

Make haste, O man, to live!
    For thou so soon must die;
Time hurries past thee like the breeze—
    How swift its moments fly!
        Make haste, O man, to live!

Make haste, O man, to do
    Whatever must be done!
Thou hast no time to lose in sloth,
    Thy day will soon be gone!
        Make haste, O man, to live!

Up then, with speed, and work;
    Fling ease and self away;
This is no time for thee to sleep,
    Up, watch, and work, and pray!
        Make haste, O man, to live!

The useful, not the great,
   The thing that never dies,
The silent toil that is not lost:
   Set these before thine eyes.
     Make haste, O man, to live!

Make haste, O man, to live!
   Thy time is almost o'er;
Oh, sleep not, dream not, but arise,
   The Judge is at the door.
     Make haste, O man, to live!

The first of these is full of sympathetic and gentle luring from earthly things; the other is a bold and manly outcry to the slumberers and lingerers. Oh that the questions in another hymn of this group, "Shall this life of mine be wasted?" could be personally presented and pressed home upon the thousands of weary, dissatisfied lives which are being wasted, when they might be filled with gladness and usefulness!

THE WASTED LIFE.

Shall this life of mine be wasted?
   Shall this vineyard lie untilled?
Shall true joy pass by untasted,
   And this soul remain unfilled!

Shall the God-given hours be scattered
   Like the leaves upon the plain?
Shall the blossoms die unwatered
   By the drops of heavenly rain?

Shall this heart still spend its treasures
   On the things that fade and die?
Shall it court the hollow pleasures
   Of bewitching vanity?

Oh that these life-wasting ones might awake to the recognition of what it is that is lacking, and thus be ready to listen to the invitation so fully yet briefly given in—

HO, YE THIRSTY! PARCHED AND FAINTING.

Ho, ye thirsty! parched and fainting,
Here are waters, turn and see!
To the thirstiest, poorest, vilest,
Without money, all is free—
Thirsty sinner!
Drink and stay not, 'tis for thee.

Ho, ye weary! toiling, burdened,
With a world of woes oppressed;
Come!—it is thy Lord invites thee,
Lay thy head upon My breast.
Weary sinner!
Come to Jesus, come and rest.

Ho, ye wounded! bruisèd, broken,
Come, and health Divine receive;
Look to Him who heals the wounded,
He alone can healing give,
Wounded sinner!
Look to Jesus, look and live!

Another group of Dr. Bonar's specialities are those bearing upon the hope of the Church, the Coming of the Lord Jesus Christ. The following three constitute a striking sequence:—

THE WAITING CHURCH.

The Church has waited long
Her absent Lord to see;
And still in loneliness she waits,
A friendless stranger she.
Age after age has gone,
Sun after sun has set,
And still in weeds of widowhood,
She weeps a mourner yet.
Come, then, Lord Jesu, come.

Saint after saint on earth
Has lived, and loved, and died,
And as they left us one by one,
We laid them side by side,
We laid them down to sleep,
But not in hope forlorn;
We laid them but to slumber there
Till the last glorious morn.
Come, then, Lord Jesu, come.

The serpent's brood increase;
The powers of hell grow bold;
The conflict thickens, faith is low,
And love is waxing cold,
How long, O Lord our God,
Holy, and true, and good!
Wilt Thou not judge Thy suffering Church,
Her sighs, and tears, and blood?
Come, then, Lord Jesu, come.

We long to hear Thy voice,
To see Thee face to face:
To share Thy crown and glory then,
As now we share Thy grace.
Come, Lord, and wipe away
The curse, the sin, the stain;
And make this blighted world of ours
Thine own fair world again.
Come, then, Lord Jesu, come.

TIME'S SUN IS FAST SETTING.

Time's sun is fast setting, its twilight is nigh:
Its evening is falling in cloud o'er the sky:
Its shadows are stretching in ominous gloom;
Its midnight approaches, the midnight of doom.
Then haste, sinner, haste, there is mercy for thee,
And wrath is preparing—flee, lingerer, flee!

Rides forth the fierce tempest on the wings of the cloud;
The moan of the night blast is fitful and loud;
The mountains are heaving, the forests are bowed,
The ocean is surging, earth gathers its shroud.
Then haste, sinner, haste, there is mercy for thee,
And wrath is preparing—flee, lingerer, flee!

The vision is nearing, the Judge and the throne!
The voice of the angel proclaims, "It is done."
On the whirl of the tempest its Ruler shall come,
And the blaze of His glory flash out from its gloom.
Then haste, sinner, haste, there is mercy for thee,
And wrath is preparing—flee, lingerer, flee!

With clouds He is coming! His people shall sing:
With gladness they hail Him Redeemer and King:
The iron rod wielding—the rod of His ire,
He cometh to kindle earth's last fatal fire.
Then haste, sinner, haste, there is mercy for thee,
And wrath is preparing—flee, lingerer, flee!

PEACE TO THE WORLD! THE LORD IS COME.

Peace to the world! the Lord is come;
   Its days of conflict now are o'er;
The Prince of Peace ascends the throne;
   And war has ceased from shore to shore!

Joy to the world! Messiah reigns!
   Earth's diadems are on His brow;
Its rebel kingdoms are become
   His everlasting kingdom now.

Rest to the nations, blessèd rest!
   The storm is hushed above, below;
Joy to creation; welcome sound
   After six thousand years of woe!

The earth again is Paradise,
   The desert blossoms as the rose:

Far happier place than Eden this:
Far brighter, sweeter days than those!

Oh, long expected, absent long,
    Star of creation's troubled gloom,
Let heaven and earth break forth in song.
    Messiah Saviour, art Thou come?

For Thou hast bought us with Thy blood,
    And Thou wast slain to set us free;
Thou mad'st us kings and priests to God,
    And we shall reign on earth with Thee!

In "The Church has waited long, her absent Lord to see," we have the
"ceaseless call, and deep desire of love," the waiting and the wearying, the "How
long, O Lord?" and the "Come, Lord Jesus!" of His own beloved and loving
ones. In the second hymn, "Time's sun is fast setting," we have a grandly awful glimpse of the majesty of "His coming to judge the world." In the third,
"Peace to the world! the Lord is come!" we have an exquisite gleam of millen-
nial peace and brightness, a deep repose of satisfaction and serene rather than
ecstatic praise. Something of the spirit of all three of these hymns is combined
in the following hymn:—

COME, LORD, AND TARRY NOT.

Come, Lord, and tarry not,
    Bring the long looked-for day;
Oh! why these years of waiting here,
    These ages of delay?

Come, for Thy saints still wait;
    Daily ascends their sigh;
The Spirit and the bride say, Come!
    Dost Thou not hear the cry?

Come, for creation groans,
    Impatient of Thy stay;
Worn out with these long years of ill,
    These ages of delay.

Come, for the corn is ripe;
    Put in Thy sickle now;
Reap the great harvest of the earth;
    Sower and Reaper Thou!

Come in Thy glorious might,
    Come with the iron rod,
Disperse Thy foes before Thy face,
    Most mighty Son of God.

Come, and make all things new;
    Build up this ruined earth;
Restore our faded paradise,
    Creation's second birth.

Come, and begin Thy reign
    Of everlasting peace:
Come, take the Kingdom to Thyself,
    Great King of Righteousness!

One more group must be illustrated, a very bright and lovely one,—the hymns which, either wholly or in part, tell of the Heavenly Home. In no direction is Dr. Bonar happier.

•   •   •   •   •

[The unfinished manuscript closes here. How could life's work itself close more fittingly than with "bright and lovely" thoughts of "the Heavenly Home"?—*The Editor of "The Day of Days."*] [1]

---

[1] This closing, bracketed note was written by Charles Bullock, who also was the editor and publisher of a number of evangelical magazines and of Home Words Publishing Office in London. He had been William Henry Havergal's curate (and then the next rector when W.H.H. resigned because of his health) at St. Nicholas Church in Worcester, knowing F.R.H. since she was a teenager, and he much valued her works, doing much to make her writings known and read both while she lived and after she died.

A Clear Small Vase.

HYMNS OF FRANCES RIDLEY HAVERGAL.

BY HER SISTER, JANE MIRIAM CRANE.

IT seems fitting that another "Specimen Glass"[1] should be added to the collection by the beloved Frances Ridley Havergal, containing a few of her own hymns gathered by a sister's hand.

Probably all modern Hymnals contain some of these hymns, so Scriptural and so elevating; there are fifty-four in "Songs of Grace and Glory," edited by the late Rev. C. B. Snepp.

Undoubtedly they take a high rank in the hymnology of the English Church; and beyond its bounds they are ministers of mercy to the wandering ones, and of revival to the members of that universal Church "which is the blessed company of all faithful people."

With respect to their diction and metre, an appreciative reviewer remarks:—"We have received at Miss Havergal's hands hymns which, for the rich qualities of their music, have not been surpassed. She has a thorough mastery of the subtleties of metre, her scanning is simply perfect, and never did dactyls and spondees render to poet a more willing service than they did to her."

Among her later sacred poems, and especially in "Life Chords," are grand and soul-inspiring flights. One of these another reviewer terms "the poetic glory of the sublime and marvellous description of 'The Thoughts of God.'" But these not being metrical "Hymns" will not be quoted here.

One of my Sister's earliest hymns was written in Germany in 1859. Coming in weary one day, she sat down before a picture of the Saviour, with the motto beneath, "I gave My life for thee": the following lines flashed upon her, and she wrote them down in pencil. On reading them over, they did not satisfy her, and she threw the paper into the fire, but it fell out unharmed. Some time after, showing them to her Father, he gave a warm approval, and they first appeared in *Good Words*.

---

[1] See the explanation on pages iv–v of this book.

" I GAVE MY LIFE FOR THEE."

I gave My life for thee,
　　My precious blood I shed
That thou might'st ransomed be,
　　And quickened from the dead.
I gave My life for thee:
What hast thou given for Me?

I spent long years for thee,
　　In weariness and woe,
That an eternity
　　Of joy thou mightest know.
I spent long years for thee:
Hast thou spent one for Me?

My Father's home of light,
　　My rainbow-circled throne,
I left, for earthly night,
　　For wanderings sad and lone.
I left it all for thee:
Hast thou left aught for Me?

I suffered much for thee,
　　More than thy tongue may tell
Of bitterest agony
　　To rescue thee from hell.
I suffered much for thee:
What canst thou bear for Me?

And I have brought to thee,
　　Down from My home above,
Salvation full and free,
　　My pardon and My love.
Great gifts I brought to thee:
What hast thou brought to Me?

Oh! let thy life be given,
　　Thy years for Him be spent;
World-fetters all be riven,
　　And joy with suffering blent.
Bring thou thy worthless all:
Follow thy Saviour's call!

This affecting appeal must have carried conviction to many a careless heart. Some years afterwards she wrote what seems like a companion hymn, describing the coming of a soul to this loving Saviour.

"I BRING MY SINS TO THEE."

I bring my sins to Thee,
    The sins I cannot count,
That all may cleansèd be
    In thy once-opened Fount.
I bring them, Saviour, all to Thee,
The burden is too great for me.

My heart to Thee I bring,
    The heart I cannot read,
A faithless wandering thing,
    An evil heart indeed.
I bring it, Saviour, now to Thee,
That fixed and faithful it may be.

To Thee I bring my care,
    The care I cannot flee,
Thou wilt not only share
    But bear it all for me.
O loving Saviour, now to Thee
I bring the load that wearies me.

I bring my grief to Thee,
    The grief I cannot tell;
No words shall needed be,
    Thou knowest all so well.
I bring the sorrow laid on me,
O suffering Saviour, now to Thee.

My joys to Thee I bring,
    The joys Thy love hath given,
That each may be a wing
    To lift me nearer heaven.
I bring them, Saviour, all to Thee,
For Thou hast purchased all for me.

My life I bring to Thee,
   I would not be my own;
O Saviour, let me be
   Thine ever, Thine alone.
My heart, my life, my all, I bring
To Thee, my Saviour and my King.

In contrast to these lines are the glowing and triumphant strains of her

ADVENT SONG.

Thou art coming, O my Saviour!
   Thou art coming, O my King!
In Thy beauty all resplendent,
In Thy glory all transcendent,
   Well may we rejoice and sing!
Coming! in the opening east,
   Herald brightness slowly swells;
Coming! O my glorious Priest,
   Hear we not Thy golden bells?

Thou art coming, Thou art coming!
   We shall meet Thee on Thy way,
We shall see Thee, we shall know Thee,
We shall bless Thee, we shall show Thee
   All our hearts could never say.
What an anthem that will be,
   Ringing out our love to Thee,
Pouring out our rapture sweet
   At Thine own all-glorious feet!

Thou art coming! Rays of glory,
   Through the veil Thy death has rent,
Touch the mountain and the river
With a golden glowing quiver,
   Thrill of light and music blent.
Earth is brightened when this gleam
   Falls on flower and rock and stream;
Life is brightened when this ray
   Falls upon its darkest day.

Not a cloud and not a shadow,
   Not a mist and not a tear,
Not a sin and not a sorrow,
Not a dim and veiled to-morrow
   For that sunrise grand and clear!
Jesus, Saviour, once with Thee,
   Nothing else seems worth a thought!
Oh, how marvellous will be
   All the bliss Thy pain hath wrought!

Thou art coming! At Thy table
   We are witnesses for this,
While remembering hearts Thou meetest,
In communion clearest, sweetest,
   Earnest of our coming bliss.
Showing not Thy death alone
   And Thy love exceeding great,
But Thy coming and Thy throne,
   All for which we long and wait.

Thou art coming! We are waiting
   With a hope that cannot fail;
Asking not the day or hour,
Resting on Thy word of power,
   Anchored safe within the veil.
Time appointed may be long,
   But the vision must be sure;
Certainty shall make us strong,
   Joyful patience can endure.

Oh, the joy to see Thee reigning,
   Thee my own belovèd Lord!
Every tongue Thy name confessing,
Worship, honour, glory, blessing,
   Brought to Thee with glad accord!
Thee, my Master and my Friend,
   Vindicated and enthroned!
Unto earth's remotest end
   Glorified, adored, and owned!

The following is a bright and comprehensive Whit-Sunday hymn :—

"TO THEE, O COMFORTER DIVINE."

To Thee, O Comforter Divine,
For all Thy grace and power benign,
> Sing we Alleluia!

To Thee, whose faithful love had place
In God's great Covenant of Grace,
> Sing we Alleluia!

To Thee, whose faithful voice doth win
The wandering from the ways of sin,
> Sing we Alleluia!

To Thee, whose faithful power doth heal,
Enlighten, sanctify, and seal,
> Sing we Alleluia!

To Thee, whose faithful truth is shown
By every promise made our own,
> Sing we Alleluia!

To Thee, our Teacher and our Friend,
Our faithful Leader to the end,
> Sing we Alleluia!

To Thee, by Jesus Christ sent down,
Of all His gifts the sum and crown,
> Sing we Alleluia!

To Thee, who art with God the Son
And God the Father ever One,
> Sing we Alleluia!

Another specimen of animating praise is on the text "Whom having not seen, ye love" (1 Peter 1:8).

"O SAVIOUR, PRECIOUS SAVIOUR!"

O Saviour, precious Saviour,
 Whom yet unseen we love,
O Name of might and favour,
 All other names above:
  We worship Thee, we bless Thee,
   To Thee alone we sing;
  We praise Thee, and confess Thee
   Our holy Lord and King!

O Bringer of salvation,
 Who wondrously hast wrought,
Thyself the revelation
 Of love beyond our thought:
  We worship Thee, we bless Thee,
   To Thee alone we sing;
  We praise Thee, and confess Thee
   Our gracious Lord and King!

In Thee all fulness dwelleth,
 All grace and power Divine:
The glory that excelleth
 O Son of God, is Thine:
  We worship Thee, we bless Thee,
   To Thee alone we sing;
  We praise Thee, and confess Thee
   Our glorious Lord and King!

O grant the consummation
 Of this our song above,
In endless adoration
 And everlasting love:
  There shall we praise and bless Thee,
   Where perfect praises ring,
  And evermore confess Thee
   Our Saviour and our King!

In a calm and tender and sweet hymn for the Holy Communion, faith and hope and love beautifully entwine around the cross!

"BENEATH HIS SHADOW."

Sit down beneath His shadow,
    And rest with great delight;
The faith that now beholds Him
    Is pledge of future sight.

Our Master's love remember,
    Exceeding great and free;
Lift up thy heart in gladness,
    For He remembers thee.

Bring every weary burden,
    Thy sin, thy fear, thy grief;
He calls the heavy laden
    And gives them kind relief.

His righteousness "all glorious"
    Thy festal robe shall be;
And love that passeth knowledge
    His banner over thee.

A little while, though parted,
    Remember, wait, and love,
Until He comes in glory,
    Until we meet above.

Till in the Father's kingdom
    The heavenly feast is spread,
And we behold His beauty,
    Whose blood for us was shed!

Readers of the "Memorials of F. R. Havergal" will remember how intensely she loved her Sunday scholars at St. Nicholas', Worcester: and to show how sweetly and simply she wrote for such little ones, a specimen is given from a volume of twelve pieces, set to music by Randegger, and dedicated to Princess Beatrice, then herself a child:—

Now the daylight goes away,
Saviour, listen while I pray,
Asking Thee to watch and keep,
And to send me quiet sleep.

Jesus, Saviour, wash away
All that has been wrong to-day;
Help me every day to be
Good and gentle, more like Thee.

Let my near and dear ones be
Always near and dear to Thee;
Oh! bring me and all I love
To Thy happy home above.

Now my evening praise I give;
Thou didst die that I might live,
All my blessings come from Thee;
Oh, how good Thou art to me!

Thou, my best and kindest Friend,
Thou wilt love me to the end;
Let me love Thee more and more,
Always better than before.

Another model of simplicity is "Seulement pour Toi!" written for the Swiss peasants of Finshaut; an account of which is given in her "Swiss Letters," where also will be found her exquisite Night-Song. I quote the latter in the hope that it may bring comfort to many sufferers.

A SONG IN THE NIGHT.

I take this pain, Lord Jesus,
    From Thine own hand,
The strength to bear it bravely
    Thou wilt command.

I am too weak for effort,
    So let me rest,
In hush of sweet submission,
    On Thine own breast.

I take this pain, Lord Jesus,
    As proof indeed
That Thou art watching closely
    My truest need:

That Thou, my Good Physician,
    Art watching still,
That all Thine own good pleasure
    Thou wilt fulfil.

I take this pain, Lord Jesus!
    What Thou dost choose
The soul that really loves Thee
    Will not refuse:

It is not for the first time
    I trust to-day;
For Thee my heart has never
    A trustless "Nay!"

I take this pain, Lord Jesus!
    But what beside?
'Tis no unmingled portion
    Thou dost provide.

In every hour of faintness,
    My cup runs o'er
With faithfulness and mercy,
    And love's sweet store.

I take this pain, Lord Jesus,
    As Thine own gift;
And true though tremulous praises
    I now uplift.

I am too weak to sing them,
    But Thou dost hear
The whisper from the pillow—
    Thou art so near!

'Tis Thy dear hand, O Saviour,
    That presseth sore,
The hand that bears the nail-prints
    For evermore.

And now beneath its shadow,
    Hidden by Thee,

The pressure only tells me
Thou lovest me!

Her ardent missionary zeal, now commemorated by "the Frances Ridley Havergal Church Missionary Memorial Fund," is exemplified in her animated and eloquent "Tell it out!" which is now often sung by assembled thousands. It was written at Winterdyne one snowy Sunday morning when unable to go to church. As she afterwards said: "In reading the Psalms for the day I came to 'Tell it out among the heathen that the Lord is King,' and I thought, what a splendid first line! and then words and music came rushing in to me." When the church-goers returned, hymn and harmonies were all beautifully written out, and then sung, in quick tune, and with the spirit which only those who heard her can imagine.

"TELL IT OUT!"

Psalm 96:10.—P. B.V. [Prayer Book Version]

Tell it out among the heathen that the Lord is King!
Tell it out! Tell it out!
Tell it out among the nations, bid them shout and sing!
Tell it out! Tell it out!
Tell it out, with adoration, that He shall increase;
That the mighty King of Glory is the King of Peace;
Tell it out with jubilation, though the waves may roar,
That He sitteth on the water-floods, our King for evermore!

Tell it out among the heathen that the Saviour reigns!
Tell it out! Tell it out!
Tell it out among the nations, bid them burst their chains.
Tell it out! Tell it out!
Tell it out among the weeping ones that Jesus lives;
Tell it out among the weary ones what rest He gives:
Tell it out among the sinners that He came to save;
Tell it out among the dying that He triumphed o'er the grave.

Tell it out among the heathen Jesus reigns above!
Tell it out! Tell it out!
Tell it out among the nations that His reign is love!
Tell it out! Tell it out!

Tell it out among the highways and the lanes at home;
Tell it out across the mountains and the ocean foam!
Like the sound of many waters let our glad shout be,
Till it echo and re-echo from the islands of the sea!

Among her hymns for special occasions, how animating is the following, and how truly "happy" would each New Year prove, if entered upon in the same spirit of fervent faith!

A NEW YEAR'S HYMN.

Isaiah 12:2.

Standing at the portal
　　Of the opening Year,
Words of comfort meet us,
　　Hushing every fear;
Spoken through the silence
　　By our Father's voice,
Tender, strong, and faithful,
　　Making us rejoice.
　　　　　Onward then, and fear not,
　　　　　　　Children of the day!
　　　　　For His word shall never,
　　　　　　　Never pass away!

I, the Lord, am with thee,
　　Be thou not afraid!
I will help and strengthen,
　　Be thou not dismayed!
Yea I will uphold thee
　　With My own right hand,
Thou art called and chosen
　　In My sight to stand.
　　　　　Onward then, and fear not, etc.

For the year before us,
　　Oh what rich supplies!
For the poor and needy
　　Living streams shall rise;

For the sad and sinful
   Shall His grace abound;
For the faint and feeble
   Perfect strength be found.
      Onward then, and fear not, etc.

He will never fail us,
   He will not forsake;
His eternal covenant
   He will never break!
Resting on His promise,
   What have we to fear?
God is all-sufficient
   For the coming year.
      Onward then, and fear not,
        Children of the day!
      For His word shall never,
        Never pass away!

The following Birthday hymn sweetly expresses prayerful hope and trust:—

"CERTAINLY I WILL BE WITH THEE."

Exodus 3:12.

"Certainly I will be with thee!" Father, I have found it true:
To Thy faithfulness and mercy I would set my seal anew.
All the year Thy grace hath kept me, Thou my help indeed hast been,
Marvellous the loving-kindness every day and hour hath seen.

"Certainly I will be with thee!" Let me feel it, Saviour dear,
Let me know that Thou art with me, very precious, very near.
On this day of solemn pausing, with Thyself all longing still,
Let Thy pardon, let Thy presence, let Thy peace my spirit fill.

"Certainly I will be with thee!" Blessèd Spirit, come to me,
Rest upon me, dwell within me, let my heart Thy temple be;
Through the trackless year before me, Holy One, with me abide!
Teach me, comfort me, and calm me, be my ever-present Guide.

"Certainly I will be with thee:" Starry promise in the night!
All uncertainties, like shadows, flee away before its light.
"Certainly I will be with thee!" He hath spoken: I have heard!
True of old, and true this moment, I will trust Jehovah's word.

The last night of a visit in a house where her loving counsels had been great-ly blessed, she was "too happy to sleep," and (she says) "these little couplets formed themselves and chimed in my heart one after another till they finished with 'Ever, *only*, ALL for Thee!'"

CONSECRATION HYMN.

"Yea, let Him take ALL."—2 Samuel 19:30.

Take my life, and let it be
Consecrated, Lord, to Thee.

Take my moments and my days,
Let them flow in ceaseless praise.

Take my hands, and let them move
At the impulse of Thy love.

Take my feet, and let them be
Swift and "beautiful" for Thee.

Take my voice, and let me sing
Always, only, for my King.

Take my lips, and let them be
Filled with messages from Thee.

Take my silver and my gold,
Not a mite would I withhold.

Take my intellect, and use
Every power as Thou shalt choose.

Take my will, and make it Thine,
It shall be no longer mine.

Take my heart, it *is* Thine own,
It shall be Thy royal throne.

Take my love; my Lord, I pour
At Thy feet its treasure-store.

Take myself, and I will be
Ever, *only*, ALL for Thee.

The later years of Frances Ridley Havergal's life were brightened by the full light of God's countenance, and she attained the greatest measure of holy joy that perhaps is ever known on earth. She entered "the country of Beulah, where the sun shineth day and night, and Doubting Castle cannot so much as be seen, where the redeemed meet with abundance of all they have sought for in their pilgrimage, and drawing near to the City, have yet a more perfect view thereof. There are the King's walks and arbours where he delighted to be," etc., and in this goodly land she wrote,—

" RESTING."

Isaiah 28:12.

Resting on the faithfulness of Christ our Lord,
Resting on the fulness of His own sure word,
Resting on His power, on His love untold,
Resting on His covenant secured of old.

Resting 'neath His guiding hand for untracked days,
Resting 'neath His shadow from the noontide rays,
Resting at the eventide beneath His wing
In the fair pavilion of our Saviour King.

Resting in the fortress while the foe is nigh,
Resting in the life-boat while the waves roll high,
Resting in His chariot for the swift glad race;
Resting, always resting in His boundless grace.

Resting in the pastures and beneath the Rock,
Resting by the waters where He leads His flock,
Resting, while we listen at His glorious feet,
Resting in His very arms! O rest complete!

Resting and believing, let us onward press,
Resting in Himself, the Lord our Righteousness,
Resting and rejoicing, let His saved ones sing,
Glory, glory, glory be to Christ our King!

One of her "Closing Chords" will fitly fill our last "Specimen Glass."

"JUST WHEN THOU WILT."

Just when Thou wilt, O Master, call!
Or at the noon, or evening fall,
Or in the dark, or in the light,—
Just when Thou wilt, it must be right.

Just when Thou wilt, O Saviour, come,
Take me to dwell in Thy bright home!
Or when the snows have crowned my head,
Or ere it hath one silver thread.

Just when Thou wilt, O Bridegroom, say,
"Rise up, my love, and come away!"
Open to me Thy golden gate,
Just when Thou wilt, or soon, or late.

Just when Thou wilt, Thy time is best,
Thou shalt appoint my hour of rest,
Marked by the Sun of perfect love,
Shining unchangeably above.

Just when Thou wilt!—no choice for me,
Life is a gift to me for Thee;
Death is a hushed and glorious tryst,
With Thee, my King, my Saviour, Christ!

And so, being, like Christiana, ready to depart, the message came, "I bring thee tidings that the Master calleth for thee, and expecteth that thou shouldst stand in His presence, in clothes of immortality, within these ten days. And the token was an arrow sharpened with love." After about "ten days'" severe illness, *singing* as she crossed the shining sands of the river of death, bright with light from heaven, my Sister entered "with exceeding joy" into the presence of the KING.

William Henry Havergal (1793–1870).

Miriam's "Specimen Glass"[1] on hymns by W.H.H. was Chapter 7 of her bi-ography, *Records of the Life of the Rev. William Henry Havergal, M.A.* (London: "Home Words" Publishing Office, 1882).

A CLEAR SMALL VASE.

HYMNS OF WILLIAM HENRY HAVERGAL.

BY HIS DAUGHTER, JANE MIRIAM CRANE.

Missionary hymns—Astley Wake Sunday—Hymns for Sunday-school sermons—Harvest hymn—The National Anthem, new version—Christmas Carols—Hymns written in illness—"Jerusalem the Golden"—"The Rock of Ages"—"My times are in Thy hand"—"Summertide is coming"—"Just as Thou wilt"—"Rest in the Lord"—Palindrome on Easter Even—"A Fireside View of Sunset."

A s the greater number of my father's hymns were written before he left Astley, the notice which is due to them is given here by the reprint and enlargement of a paper which appeared in *The Day of Days* magazine for March and April, 1882—

It was the intention of my lamented sister, Frances Ridley Havergal, to write a concluding chapter of "Specimen Glasses"[1] on the hymns of her father. The Editor of *The Day of Days* has asked me to prepare such a paper, and in doing so I have chosen for notice some of the hymns which I think she would have been likely to select.

From his boyhood my father was fond of rhyming, chiefly with a view to amuse and brighten his own home circle; and even in his riper years many were the poetical and playful epistles to his young friends, and acrostics on their names.

His hymns seem almost invariably to have been called forth by special oc-casions; and many of these were printed on hand-bills (as was formerly the cus-tom), to be sung at the annual sermons for the Church Missionary Society, in his beloved church of Astley, Worcestershire. He always composed a tune for each new hymn. It should be remembered that these were times when but few missionary hymns had been written, and the deep interest he took in Missionary work was very exceptional. Fifty or sixty years ago a missionary sermon would have been considered in many of our churches no slight innovation.

---

[1] See the explanation on pages iv–v of this book.

A specimen hymn, simple yet spirited, is given, which was sung, after a sermon by the Rev. I. Lamb, D.D., Master of Corpus Christi College, Cambridge, on the 23rd of September, 1827, when nearly £21 was collected—a goodly sum for a country congregation.

"HERALDS OF THE LORD OF GLORY."

"Say (Tell it out) among the heathen, that the Lord reigneth."—Psalm 96:10.

> Heralds of the Lord of glory!
>   Lift your voices, lift them high;
> Tell the Gospel's wondrous story,
>   Tell it fully, faithfully;
> Tell the heathen 'midst their woe,
> Jesus reigns, above, below.
>
> Haste the day, the bright, the glorious!
>   When the sad and sin-bound slave
> High shall laud in pealing chorus
>   Him who reigns, and reigns to save.
> Tempter, tremble! Idols, fall!
> Jesus reigns, the Lord of all!
>
> Christians! send to joyless regions
>   Heralds of the gladdening word,
> Let them, voiced like trumpet-legions,
>   Preach the kingdom of the Lord:
> Tell the heathen—Jesus died!
> Reigns He now, though crucified.
>
> Saviour, let Thy quickening Spirit
>   Touch each herald-lip with fire,
> Nations then shall own Thy merit,
>   Hearts shall glow with Thy desire,
> Earth in jubilee shall sing.
> Jesus reigns, the eternal King.

Several of the most poetical and popular of his missionary hymns are the following. The first was a special favourite with his daughter, Frances Ridley Havergal.

"SHOUT, O EARTH! FROM SILENCE WAKING."

"And men shall be blessed in Him: all nations shall call Him blessed."—Psalm 72:17.

Shout, O earth! from silence waking,
    Tune with joy thy varied tongue;
Shout! as when, from chaos breaking,
    Sweetly flowed thy natal song:
Shout! for thy Creator's love
Sends redemption from above.

Downward from His star-paved dwelling
    Comes the incarnate Son of God;
Countless voices, thrilling, swelling,
    Tell the triumphs of His blood:
Shout! He comes thy tribes to bless
With His spotless righteousness.

See His glowing hand uplifted!
    Clustering bounties drop around;
Rebels e'en are richly gifted,
    Pardon, peace, and joy abound!
Shout, O earth! and let thy song
Ring the vaulted heavens along.

Call Him blessèd on thy mountains,
    In thy wilds and citied plains;
Call Him blessèd where thy fountains
    Speak in softly murmuring strains.
Let thy captives, let thy kings
Join thy lyre of thousand strings.

Blessed Lord, and Lord of blessing!
    Pour Thy quickening gifts abroad;
Raptured tongues, Thy love confessing,
    Shall extol the living God.
Blessed, blessed, blessed Lord!
Heaven shall chant no other word.

THE LIGHT OF LIFE.

"In Him was life; and the life was the light of men." John 1:4

In doubt and dread dismay,
'Midst Superstition's gloom;
The heathen grope their way,
And joyless reach the tomb:
    No holy light,
    No balmy ray
    Of Gospel-day
    Has blessed their sight.

Then, Star of Life, arise!
And on thy healing wing,
With blood of sacrifice,
Thy great salvation bring:
    Let heathen lands
    Thy brightness see:
    Oh set them free
    From cruel bands.

With searching beam explore
The dark strongholds of sin:
And on the prisoners pour
Transforming light within.
    Bright morning Star!
    Unveil thy face,
    And shed thy grace,
    In realms afar.

O Jesu, Light of Life!
Arouse the world from sleep;
Send holy love in place of strife,
And joy to those who weep.
    Great King of Kings!
    Thy Spirit give!
    Let Gentiles live,
    Beneath thy wings.

" CHRISTIANS, HASTE ! THE MORN IS BREAKING."

"Until the day dawn, and the Day-star arise."—2 Peter 1:19.

Widely 'midst the slumbering nations,
 Darkness holds his despot sway;
Cruel in his habitations,
 Ruthless o'er his prostrate prey.
 Star of Bethlehem!
Rise and beam in conquering day!

Light of Life, our sole Defender,
 Rise, with healing on Thy wing;
Rise, in all Thy soothing splendour;
 Rise, and earth with joy shall sing!
 Israel's Glory!
Gentiles call Thee "Lord and King!"

Christians, haste! the morn is breaking;
 Darkness wheels his downward flight;
But, your polished armour taking,
 Stand! nor quit the waning fight.
 Great Redeemer!
Guard us with Thy shield of light.

Onward, Christians, onward pressing,
 Triumph in the Crucified!
Endless honour, rest, and blessing,
 Wait you at His radiant side.
 Cease not, cease not,
Till you see Him glorified!

" NO DAWN OF HOLY LIGHT."

"The Dayspring from on high hath visited us, to give light to them that sit in darkness, and in the shadow of death."—Luke 1:78, 79.

"To turn men from darkness to light, and from the power of Satan unto God."—Acts 26:18.

"I am the Light of the world."—John 8:11.

No dawn of holy light,
No day of sacred rest,
E'er breaks upon the heathen's sight,
To soothe his troubled breast.

But lo! with healing ray,
The Dayspring meets our eye:
And Christians, on their Master's day,
Rejoice to feel Him nigh.

To Him let praise be given,
The noblest, sweetest, best;
For He has brought us light from heaven,
And hope of endless rest.

Lord, let Thy saving light,
Thy day of glorious rest,
Soon chase from earth the toilsome night
And soothe each wearied breast!

REDEMPTION.

"Who gave himself a ransom for all, to be testified in due time."—I Timothy 2:6.

Redemption! Oh the thrilling word!
    It tells of joy in woe;
Of more than prophets saw or heard,
    Of all that *we* can know.

Redemption! God's great charity
    To man imprisoned long;
The world's reprieve; the sinner's plea;
    And heaven's eternal song.

Redemption! but—its countless cost!
    It cost the blood of Him
Who spread the heavens, and rules the host
    Of flaming Seraphim.

Redemption! be its joy proclaimed
    By men of every tongue,

Where Christ has never yet been named,
Where Satan's power is strong.

REDEEMER, Thou who diedst *for all!*
Let all Thy love adore:
Let Jew and Heathen join to call
Thee—*Lord* for evermore!

" BRIGHTER THAN MERIDIAN SPLENDOUR."

"The Sun of Righteousness."—Malachi 4:2.

Brighter than meridian splendour,
  Beams Messiah's spotless fame;
Him we hail our firm Defender,
  Him let every tongue proclaim.
      He is precious,
      He is gracious,
  He for ever is the same.

Lord of glory! Source of favour!
  Bid Thy heralds take their stand:
Let Thy name's reviving savour
  Wake each dark and drowsy land.
      Saviour, hear us;
      Speak and cheer us,
  When we lift the suppliant hand.

Thou art all! and all adore Thee,
  Where they hymn one ceaseless song:
Soon shall earth, subdued before Thee,
  Peal Thy name her tribes among.
      Sons of glory,
      Chant the story,
  And your deep Amen prolong!

For several years the Church Missionary sermons were preached on the Astley Wake Sunday, a day my Father was anxious to redeem from the intemperance and revelling with which it was kept; and the first hymn at the morning service was always the following, which he wrote in 1834. The notes accompanying the hymn are subjoined.

ASTLEY WAKE.

Many persons require to be informed, and others to be reminded, that a parish Wake is properly a Religious Festival. It was originally the Feast of the Dedication of the Parish Church; and was kept by watching, or waking, unto prayer and praise, during the whole of the preceding night, till sunrise.

" Blow up the trumpet in the new moon, in the time appointed, on our solemn feast-day."—Psalm 81:3.

Our festal morn is come,
    And, Lord, we come to Thee;
Thy house shall be our joyful home,
    Thy name our melody.

" These temples of Thy grace,
    How beautiful they stand!
The honours of our native place,
    And bulwarks of our land." [1]

Our fathers built this fane,[2]
    And watched the livelong night:
They sleep in death; but we remain
    To hail a purer light.

Then blow the trumpet, blow:
    The psalm, the psaltery take:
Let every heart with praise o'erflow,
    And every lip awake.

Sound, sound that sweetest strain,
    The gospel-jubilee,
Till, bursting from their idol-chain,
    The heathen shall be free.

Thus let us keep the feast,
    Thus wake to righteousness:
And teach the world, from sin released,
    The Lord our God to bless.

[1] The second verse is quoted from Dr. Watts.
[2] A "fane" was a temple.

"In the Jewish Church, notice was given of feasts, jubilees, etc., by sound of trumpet. We have now our religious feast-days. On these and all other solemn occasions, let the evangelical trumpet give a sound of victory over death, of liberty from sin, of joy and rejoicing in Christ Jesus our Saviour."—*Bishop Horne*.

My Father delighted to sing to children, and with them, his own nursery rhymes, and short hymns suited to their understanding.

He led the child-singers in Astley Church with his singularly sweet and penetrating voice, accompanying on his seraphine (a precursor of the harmoniums of to-day).

From the hymns he wrote for the annual Sunday-school sermons, three are selected. The first two are sweet and tender strains; the other a song of spiritual and inspiriting praise.

THE HOLY CHILD.

"He was subject unto them."—Luke 2:51.

Blessed Jesus, Lord and Brother,
    Once thou wast a lowly child,
Subject to Thy Virgin-mother,
    "Holy, harmless, undefiled";
Wisdom, favour, grace, and truth,
Graced, like morning stars, Thy youth.

Great Redeemer, Mediator!
    Now Thou art enthroned in light;
But Thou wearest still our nature,
    And all heaven admires the sight.
Lord, to tender years impart
Mercy's boon, the tender heart.

Jesu, by Thy childhood's favour,
    By Thy manhood's agony,
Fill us with Thy Spirit's savour,
    Train us for eternity;
With the glittering hosts above,
May we sing Thy boundless love!

THE GOOD SHEPHERD.

He shall gather the lambs with His arm, and carry them in His bosom "
—Isaiah 40:11.

To praise our Shepherd's care,
   His wisdom, love, and might;
Your loudest, loftiest songs prepare,
   And bid the world unite!

Supremely good and great,
   He tends His blood-fought fold;
He stoops, though throned in highest state,
   The feeblest to uphold.

He hears their softest plaint,
   He eyes them when they roam;
And if His meanest lamb should faint,
   His bosom bears it home.

Kind Shepherd of the sheep!
   A weakly flock are we,
And snares and foes are nigh; but keep
   The lambs who look to Thee.

And if through death's dark vale
   Our feet should early tread;
Oh, may we reach Thy fold, and hail
   The love which safely led!

"HOSANNA!"

"Hosanna to the Son of David."—Matthew 21:15, 16.

Hosanna! raise the pealing hymn
   To David's Son and Lord;
With Cherubim and Seraphim
   Exalt the Incarnate Word.

Hosanna! Lord, our feeble tongue
   No lofty strains can raise:

But Thou wilt not despise the young
 Who meekly chant Thy praise.

Hosanna! Sovereign, Prophet, Priest,
 How vast Thy gifts, how free!
Thy blood, our life: Thy word; our feast;
 Thy name, our only plea.

Hosanna! Master, lo! we bring
 Our offerings to Thy throne;
Not gold, not myrrh, nor mortal thing,
 But hearts to be Thine own.

Hosanna! once Thy gracious ear
 Approved a lisping throng;
Be gracious still, and deign to hear
 Our poor but grateful song.

O Saviour! if, redeemed by Thee,
 Thy temple we behold,
Hosannas through eternity
 We'll sing to harps of gold!

Among hymns composed for parochial occasions, a Harvest Hymn, written in 1863, for his parish of Shareshill, Staffordshire, is truly admirable for its doctrinal and practical character—

HARVEST HYMN.

"He will gather His wheat into the garner."—Matthew 3:12.

Our faithful God hath sent us
 A fruitful harvest-tide;
He summer boons hath lent us,
 And winter wants supplied.

The fields, at His ordaining,
 Stand thick with golden sheaves;
And man, full oft complaining,
 New bounty now receives.

Though Mercy largely giveth,
   Is justice pacified?
We live through Him who liveth,
   The "Corn of Wheat" that died.

Then full be our thanksgiving,
   And clear each note of joy;
While faith and holy living
   Our earnest thoughts employ.

And at the last great reaping,
   When Christ His sheaves will own,
May we, no longer weeping,
   Be garnered near His throne.

Praise we the Godhead-Union,
   The Eternal Three in One;
With them may our communion
   For ever be begun.

My father's strong feeling of loyalty was shown by versions of our National Anthem in language more graceful and becoming than

"Confound their politics,
   Frustrate their knavish tricks."

Those on the Coronation and Widowhood of the Queen, the Marriage of the Prince of Wales, and for the Festivals of the St. Nicholas Sunday-schools, at Worcester, are worthy of reprint for similar occasions.

THE NATIONAL ANTHEM.

NEW VERSION FOR THE SCHOOLS ASSEMBLING IN WORCESTER CATHEDRAL ON WHIT-MONDAY.

God save our noble Queen;
Long live Old England's Queen;
   God save the Queen!
Great and victorious,
Happy and glorious,

May she reign over us:
    God save the Queen!

On her anointed head,
All choicest blessings shed
    Forth from Thy hand:
Let her be Thy delight;
Make her path always bright;
And in Thy Word and might,
    Firm be her stand!

While nations rage and groan,
Stablish her sacred throne
    In sure repose:
Where'er our banners wave
O'er land or ocean-cave,
There all our warriors save:
    Forgive our foes!

Send peace in this our time;
Spare us from strife and crime;
    Strengthen each band!
Nursed by our gracious Queen,
May our Church e'er be seen
Planted, like evergreen
    Throughout the land.

Sovereign of earth and sky,
Hear Thou our Nation's cry,
    Bless, bless our Queen!
Grant us, through her, to be,
In Thee and all for Thee,
"Great, glorious, and free:"
    God save the Queen!

The following verses were composed on the death of the Prince Consort. My father's arrangement of the National Anthem in the minor key is, I believe, unique.

"WEEP WITH OUR QUEEN."

Let Britain's prayer ascend,
Let mournful voices blend,
    Weep with our Queen!
God of our country, see
How England bows the knee,
How suppliants cry to Thee,
    God save the Queen!

In sorrow's withering hour,
When droops the smitten flower,
    Be Thy might seen:
God of the bleeding heart,
Heal Thou the bitter smart,
Thy Spirit's grace impart,
    Comfort our Queen!

Chase every cloud away,
Turn all her night to day,
    Bright but serene:
God of the widow, hear,
Dry up her burning tear,
Strong for her help appear;
    God save the Queen!

Lord, let Thy husband-arm
Be her life's heavenly charm,
    Felt, though unseen:
Long as her days extend,
Her home and throne defend,
And give a glorious end;
    God save the Queen!

While he was Rector of St. Nicholas, musical and poetical compositions were a great resource in his failing eyesight, for which he twice obtained leave of absence to be under the care of the great Prussian oculist, Dr. de Leuw, at Gräfrath.

Writing from Langen Schwalbach, in May, 1862, my father says:—"My version of 'God save the Queen,' in the minor key, makes its way in the good-will of the loyal and musical here and in Prussia, where the tune is claimed as a native and national melody; the minorizing is much liked, no one seems to have thought of thus treating it."

My father wrote some lively Christmas Carols, the first published being:—

THE WORCESTERSHIRE CHRISTMAS CAROL.

"The glory of the Lord shone round about them."—Luke 2:9.

How grand and how bright
That wonderful night,
When angels to Bethlehem came!
They burst forth like fires,
They struck their gold lyres,
And mingled their sound with the flame.

The shepherds were 'mazed,
The pretty lambs gazed
At darkness thus turned into light:
No voice was there heard
From man, beast, or bird,
So sudden and solemn the sight.

And then, when the sound
Re-echoed around,
The hills and the dales all awoke:
The moon and the stars
Stopped their fiery cars,
And listened while Gabriel spoke:

"I bring you," said he,
"From the Glorious Three,
Good tidings to gladden mankind;
The Saviour is born,
But He lies all forlorn
In a manger, as soon you will find."

At mention of this,
(The source of all bliss),
The angels sang loudly and long,
They soared to the sky,
Beyond mortal eye,
But left us the words of their song:

"All glory to God,"
Who laid by His rod,
To smile on the world through His Son;
"And Peace be on earth,"
For this wonderful birth
Most wonderful conquests has won:

"And Good-will to man,"
Though his life's but a span,
And his thoughts all evil and wrong:
Then pray, Christians, pray;
But let Christmas-Day
Have your sweetest and holiest song.

Another favourite carol is "A Bethlehem Shepherd-Boy's Tale," in which, with unconscious poetic feeling, the child describes his unusually good thoughts and pleasant feelings through the previous day, with which the sights and sounds of Nature seem in unison, and he feels as if this must be the prelude to something uncommon. Then he describes the calm loveliness of the night, the "musical breeze" of distant angel-notes, the sudden blaze, the heavenly message, and the walk to Bethlehem to see the wonderful Babe.

A BETHLEHEM SHEPHERD-BOY'S TALE.

"Those things which were told by the shepherds."—Luke 2:18.

So happy all the day
Had I been without play;
And such good thoughts had come o'er my mind:
That I wondered what it meant,
Or for why it was sent;
As I ne'er had felt aught of the kind.

And the birds, all day long,
Had kept trilling their song;
And the sun had gone down, oh so red!
We had folded the sheep,
And were talking of sleep,
But, somehow, we cared not for bed.

The stars were all drest
In their brightest and best;
And the moon showed a streak of her gold:
'Twas a glorious night;
And we thought of the sight
Of which David our father has told.

A sound struck our ear,
Sweet, joyous, and clear,
It seemed like a musical breeze:
But, ere we could gaze,
We were all in a blaze,
And found ourselves down on our knees.

A bright one then said,
('Twas like life from the dead),
"Good tidings, good tidings I bring!
Messiah's come down;
In your own little town
You will find Him a Babe and a King!"

And then the whole choir,
Rising higher and higher,
Sang of "glory, sweet peace, and good-will,"
The sheep seemed to dance,
And the mountains to prance,
And the stars could no longer stand still.

Then onward we sped,
To find out the bed,
Where the Saviour in lowliness lay:
Near Bethlehem's inn,
(Oh shame on their sin!)
We found Him midst cattle and hay.

But we saw the blest sight;
'Twas our Judah's delight;
And Mary and Joseph were there:
And soon we made known
To all in the town
What we heard the good angel declare.

And now, every day,
I sing and I pray
To the Babe who is Saviour and all:
May His wonderful birth
Be known through the earth,
And cheer both the great and the small!

The last Carol he composed is also original in idea. A shepherd who had seen "the glory of the Lord," and heard the melody of the "heavenly host," calls upon his companions to celebrate with prayer and song the first anniversary of the Saviour's birth.

THE FIRST ANNIVERSARY OF CHRISTMAS.[1]

Come, shepherds, come, 'tis just a year
Since sweetest music woke our ear,
    And angels blessed our sight.
Come, lift your heart, and tune your voice,
And bid the hills and vales rejoice,
    As on that glorious night.

'Tis just a year ago, we say,
When night shone out as clear as day,
    And Heaven came down to earth.
How we did fear, how we did gaze,
Surrounded by the sudden blaze,
    And thrilled with sounds of mirth!

Ah! see you not that angel-choir?
And hear you not that mighty lyre

---

[1] For the words and music of these Carols, see the Musical Editions of "Songs of Grace and Glory" (J. Nisbet & Co., 21, Berners Street).

Which hushed our bleating sheep?
And, oh, that voice of sweetest awe,
Which told us all we after saw;
   Who now would silence keep?

Come, shepherds, come, with prayer and song,
This night to be remembered long,
   Rejoice to celebrate.
With reedy pipe chant forth who can
To God all glory, love to man,
   And peace in every gate!

'Tis just a year ago to-night,
From heaven came down the Prince of Light,
   Our guilty world to bless.
Let Gentiles now with Israel sing
Our Saviour, Brother, Friend, and King,
   Our promised righteousness!

From a manuscript volume, entitled,"Forty Hymns from Subjects in the book of Genesis," written at Langen Schwalbach during a season of illness, in August and September, 1865, I transcribe the two following:—

" IS ANYTHING TOO HARD FOR HIM ? "

"Is anything too hard for the Lord?"—Genesis 18:14.

Is anything too hard for Him,
Whom Cherubim and Seraphim
   Incessantly adore?
No! He, the everlasting Son,
Made countless worlds their course to run,
   And reigneth evermore.

He stooped from highest heaven and died,
That every want might be supplied
   Of all who own His power.
His gracious eye, His mighty hand,
Are always waiting faith's command,
   In trial's darkest hour.

He can the hardest heart subdue,
The most corrupted soul renew,
   The driest bones make live;
He can the bruisèd reed bind up,
The bitter take from every cup,
   And strength to weakness give.

Then blessèd be Thy glorious might,
Thou God-man! Saviour! Infinite!
   Whom Abram longed to see,
When by Thy arm we rise from death
Our chant shall be, with ceaseless breath,
   Nought was too hard for Thee!

BETHEL

"And he called the name of that place Bethel."—Genesis 28:19.

Lonely wilds and woodland mazes,
   Spots remote from human din,
God can make His holy places,
   And reveal himself therein:
     Dread Jehovah,
   Contrite hearts Thou dwellest in.

Jacob weary, sad, and fearful,
   Chose a spot for sleep by night:
All was soon divinely cheerful,
   Heavenly visions blessed his sight;
     Henceforth Bethel
   Was his watchword and delight.

Everywhere, good Lord, be near us,
   Let us many a Bethel see;
By Thy one great vision cheer us,
   Christ the Ladder-Path to Thee,
     Gate of heaven
   Now to all believers free.

God of Jacob, God of Jesus,
 Standing at the ladder's height,
Soon from pilgrim toils release us,
 Rest us in Thy home of light:
  Blessèd Saviour,
  Thine the glory, ours the sight!

The next hymn is one rich in comfort to the tried believer.

"O CAST ON CHRIST YOUR MIGHTY CARE."

"Casting all your care upon Him, for He careth for you."—1 Peter 5:7.

O cast on Christ your mighty care,
 However great it be;
He knows it well, and can prepare
 Some sure relief for thee.

Thy surging thoughts and spectral fears
 Thy boding dreams of ill,
Thy sighings, and Thy silent tears,
 Are all within His will.

Lay these upon His holy arm,
 For He can all sustain:
He'll end thy cares, as with a charm,
 And lift thee up again.

Sustaining grace waits His command,
 And He awaits thy call;
Then pray, and down within thine hand
 Shall strength and comfort fall.

I, Lord, would cast on Thee my care,
 And nothing anxious be;
Content if Thou, who hearest prayer,
 Wilt care, O Lord, for me.

The following beautifully worded hymn will, I think, bear comparison with the well-known versions of the ancient hymn by Bernard de Morlaix on the heavenly Jerusalem.[1]

REVELATION 21.

Jerusalem the Golden
   The home of saints shall be;
What eyes have not beholden,
   They shall for ever see!
Those gem-built walls of wonder,
   Those pearly gates of praise,
Those harps of sweetest thunder,
   Those streets of sunless blaze.

By them shall Christ in glory
   Be always seen and heard,
And His Redemption-story
   Shall be their household word.
Apostles, prophets, martyrs,
   Shall their companions be,
And loved ones shall be partners
   Of their felicity.

Each golden street and dwelling
   Shall teem with happy throngs,
In holiness excelling,
   And chanting lofty songs:
The Lamb! the Lamb, once dying,
   They worship on His throne,
And fall before Him crying,
   Thou, Thou art Lord alone!

Great Bridegroom of the City,
   The Maker, Lord, and Light,
Grant us, in tender pity,
   To walk with Thee in white!

---

[1] The comparison is, we think, considerably in favour of Canon Havergal's hymn. Much that is "fanciful" in this case gives place to the substantial and the real, and there is no falling off in poetic power.—THE EDITOR OF *The Day of Days*. [The editor was Rev. Charles Bullock.]

So while on earth we linger,
All joyous in thy love,
Our hearts shall watch Thy finger
To beckon us above.

Toplady's immortal hymn, "The Rock of Ages," *seemed* to my father to confound the rock which Moses smote for water (Exodus 17:6) with the rock in which he was hidden for shelter (Exodus 33:22). Each separate case, he thought, suggested a separate train of ideas. This led him to write the next hymn.

"THE ROCK OF AGES."

PART I.

"Rock of Ages, cleft for me,
Let me hide myself in Thee,"
While the glory passeth by,
Keep me as the tenderest eye:
Keep me, for I dare not gaze
On that glory's awful blaze:
All unholy and impure,
I its light cannot endure.

When my sins, a mighty sum,
Threaten me with wrath to come:
When, to crush me, draweth near
Tyrant Doubt, or giant Fear;
When my hopes, now few and faint,
Seem to mark the almost saint:
Rock of Ages, unto Thee
I for instant shelter flee.

Rock of Ages, in Thy side
Let me joyfully abide:
Then my daily boast shall be,
Thine, Incarnate Deity:
Then no wily tempter's skill
Shall entangle me with ill:
Then nor earth nor hell shall harm,
Thou wilt shield from all alarm.

Rock of Ages, cleft for me,
Cleft from all eternity;
Hidden here, I fully share
All the Father's love and care:
Hidden here, the Spirit's might
Shall my darkness turn to light;
Rock of Ages, one with Thee,
All Thy glory I shall see.

PART II.

Rock of Ages, cleft for all,
Who for saving shelter call,
Who, forsaking selfish pride,
Stoop to enter and abide.
Cleft for all! Oh joyous sound!
Chant it long and loud around:
All may thither now repair:
Mercy meets the sinner there.

Rock of Ages, Rock of God,
Smitten not by human rod:
Opened from eternity,
Heaven's profoundest mystery!
Hidden in its wondrous cleft,
Though of all things else bereft,
Sinners find a mine of wealth,
Riches, honour, endless health.

Rock of Ages, Christ my Lord,
Hidden here, by faith's accord,
Guilty souls at once possess
Pardon, peace, and righteousness,
Though thy glory passeth by,
They may gaze and yet not die:
Yea, thy glory they shall see
In its full intensity.

Rock of Ages, Rock of Life,
Hide me in the last dread strife:

And when suns shall cease to roll,
Let thy life light up my soul!
Then, as all things pass away,
Let my raptured spirit say,
"Rock of Ages, cleft for me,"
Ever shall I dwell with Thee.

The next two hymns have been much appreciated, and well illustrate the devotional and cheerful spirit of the writer.

"MY TIMES ARE IN THY HAND."

"My times are in Thy hand,"
    Their best and fittest place;
I would not have them at command
    Without Thy guiding grace.

"My times," and yet not mine;
    I cannot them ordain;
Not one e'er waits from me a sign,
    Nor can I one detain.

"My times," O Lord, are Thine,
    And Thine their oversight:
Thy wisdom, love, and power combine
    To make them dark or bright.

I know not what shall be,
    When passing times are fled;
But all events I leave with Thee,
    And calmly bow my head.

Hence, Lord, in Thee I rest,
    And wait Thy holy will:
I lean upon my Saviour's breast,
    Or gladly go on still.

And when my "times" shall cease,
    And life shall fade away,
Then bid me, Lord, depart in peace
    To realms of endless day.

" SUMMERTIDE IS COMING."

Summer-tide is coming,
  With all its pleasant things:
Every bee is humming,
  And every songster sings.
Mornings now are brightsome,
  Inviting student thought;
Evenings too are lightsome,
  With balmy quiet fraught.
Hearths no longer lure us,
  The fields instead we roam;
Hearts albeit insure us
  A happy, happy home.

Summer-tide, I hail thee,
  The empress of the year!
But thou soon wouldst fail me,
  Were not thy Maker near.
He thy course disposes,
  Thy light, thy scent, thy glow;
He tints all thy roses,
  And paints thy brilliant bow.
Laud Him, all creation,
  The sinner's mighty Friend:
Near him be our station,
  Where summer ne'er shall end.

Among the pieces my father wrote of a more experimental kind, I quote one which was dictated in severe illness in 1860. It was apparently an impromptu; and the occasion—a sigh. Being asked if it arose from any fresh pain, he replied: "Oh, no! I feel it a little relief; but do not think I repine: I should be ashamed. Repine? No, nor change aught, though suns and stars were mine. How busy are my heart and brain!" He then repeated in whispers the following "specimen" of complete resignation.

"JUST AS THOU WILT!"

Just as Thou wilt, O Lord, do Thou!
I to Thy sovereign purpose bow;

On brightest day or darkest night
　　Whate'er is Thine is right.

Just as Thou wilt! O Lord, perform
Thy counsels 'midst the raging storm;
Not for the earth would I complain
　　Of sorrow, cross, or pain.

Just as Thou wilt! Be all to me,
E'en when Thy hand smites heavily;
Not for the stars would I repine,
　　If only Thou art mine.

Just as Thou wilt! Should anguish fierce
With scorpion stings my body pierce,
I'll praise Thee, if on me Thou'lt shine
　　And whisper, I AM thine!

Just as Thou wilt! In death's dark hour,
Should Satan's cloud around me lower,
If Thou, O Christ, wilt be my Guide,
　　No ill can me betide.

Just as Thou wilt! When Thou shalt come
And take of souls the mighty sum,
Then, blessèd Saviour, let mine be
　　Among Thy family!

Another hymn, written at the same time, is entitled

"REST IN THE LORD."

"Rest in the Lord."—Psalm 37:7.

"Rest in the Lord!" Sweet word of truth,
A word for age, a word for youth,
A word for all the weary world,
A banner-word by love unfurled.

Then cease, ye wearied ones of earth,
To slave for pleasure, gain, or mirth;

Cast down your load of vanities,
And welcome God's realities.

"Rest in the Lord!" Sweet word of grace,
To all the Saviour's new-born race;
'Tis music, light, and balm to them,
An hourly guiding apothegm.

Then, Lord of rest, we rest in Thee,
For all our daily destiny;
Our mighty guilt, our grief, our care,
We cast (strange act!) on Thee to bear.

For Thou, dear Lamb of God, wast slain,
To bear each load, and ease each pain;
And now Thy blood and righteousness
Are rocks of rest in all distress.

And when at last we fall on sleep,
Nor heart shall throb, nor eye shall weep;
Then, blessèd Saviour, let it be,
That Thou shalt write, "They rest in Me!"

Some years after this illness he felt obliged to give up parochial work, and obtained leave of absence from Shareshill. In the autumn of 1867 he bought a house at Leamington, and called it Pyrmont Villa, after his favourite resort in Germany. This was his last home; but he was able to return to Pyrmont, and take Sunday services for the English visitors in the summer of 1869.

The last lines he composed, and which he set to a Palindrome on Easter Even, 1870, are these:—

Messiah, Redeemer!
Send out Thy saving light;
Where rules the prince of night,
Day-star rise!
Cheer all eyes!

Earlier in the day he had composed the beautiful tune "Havergal," No. 163 in "Havergal's Psalmody." On Easter-Day he was seized with apoplexy, and remained unconscious forty-eight hours, when he quietly passed through death into life eternal the 19th of April, 1870.

One of his lovely little pieces in "Fireside Music" will fitly close this list of "Specimens."

A FIRESIDE VIEW OF SUNSET.

How calmly sinks the sun
Beneath the western deep,
When day his giant course has run,
And storm is hushed to sleep.

So, like the sun, would I
In tranquil eve descend,
And watch with softly waning eye
The footsteps of the end.

But though in darkness set,
The sun seems lost awhile;
He will his shroud shake off, and yet
Arise with joyous smile.

Thus, like the sun, may I
Descend to rise again,
And meet my Saviour in the sky,
With all His glorious train.

This is the book cover of the finalized edition of Songs of Grace and Glory *(London: James Nisbet & Co., 1880), more than 1,100 hymns, edited by Charles Busbridge Snepp (words) and F.R.H. (music). Frances prepared almost all of the music scores in this hymnal.*

"The Ministry of Song" was the second poem in Frances Ridley Havergal's first published book, which has the same name, *The Ministry of Song*.

The Ministry of Song.

Prelude.

AMID the broken waters of our ever-restless thought,
Oh be my verse an answering gleam from higher radiance caught;
That where through dark o'erarching boughs of sorrow, doubt, and sin,
The glorious Star of Bethlehem upon the flood looks in,
Its tiny trembling ray may bid some downcast vision turn
To that enkindling Light, for which all earthly shadows yearn.
Oh be my verse a hidden stream, which silently may flow
Where drooping leaf and thirsty flower in lonely valleys grow;
And often by its shady course to pilgrim hearts be brought
The quiet and refreshment of an upward-pointing thought;
Till, blending with the broad bright stream of sanctified endeavour,
God's glory be its ocean home, the end it seeketh ever.

The Ministry of Song.

IN God's great field of labour
    All work is not the same;
He hath a service for each one
    Who loves His holy name.
And you, to whom the secrets
    Of all sweet sounds are known,
Rise up! for He hath called you
    To a mission of your own.
And, rightly to fulfil it,
    His grace can make you strong,
Who to your charge hath given
    The Ministry of Song.

Sing to the little children,
    And they will listen well;
Sing grand and holy music,
    For they can feel its spell.

Tell them the tale of Jephthah;
    Then sing them what he said,—
'Deeper and deeper still,' and watch
    How the little cheek grows red,
And the little breath comes quicker:
    They will ne'er forget the tale,
Which the song has fastened surely,
    As with a golden nail.

I remember, late one evening,
    How the music stopped, for, hark!
Charlie's nursery door was open,
    He was calling in the dark,—
'Oh no! I am not frightened,
    And I do not want a light;
But I cannot sleep for thinking
    Of the song you sang last night.
Something about a "valley,"
    And "make rough places plain,"
And "Comfort ye;" so beautiful!
    Oh, sing it me again!'

Sing at the cottage bedside;
    They have no music there,
And the voice of praise is silent
    After the voice of prayer.
Sing of the gentle Saviour
    In the simplest hymns you know,
And the pain-dimmed eye will brighten
    As the soothing verses flow.
Better than loudest plaudits
    The murmured thanks of such,
For the King will stoop to crown them
    With His gracious 'Inasmuch.'

Sing, where the full-toned organ
    Resounds through aisle and nave,
And the choral praise ascendeth
    In concord sweet and grave.
Sing, where the village voices
    Fall harshly on your ear;
And, while more earnestly you join,
    Less discord you will hear.

The noblest and the humblest
    Alike are ' common praise,'
And not for human ear alone
    The psalm and hymn we raise.

Sing in the deepening twilight,
    When the shadow of eve is nigh,
And her purple and golden pinions
    Fold o'er the western sky.
Sing in the silver silence,
    While the first moonbeams fall;
So shall your power be greater
    Over the hearts of all.
Sing till you bear them with you
    Into a holy calm,
And the sacred tones have scattered
    Manna, and myrrh, and balm.

Sing! that your song may gladden;
    Sing like the happy rills,
Leaping in sparkling blessing
    Fresh from the breezy hills.
Sing! that your song may silence
    The folly and the jest,
And the ' idle word' be banished
    As an unwelcome guest.
Sing! that your song may echo
    After the strain is past,
A link of the love-wrought cable
    That holds some vessel fast.

Sing to the tired and anxious
    It is yours to fling a ray,
Passing indeed, but cheering,
    Across the rugged way.
Sing to God's holy servants,
    Weary with loving toil,
Spent with their faithful labour
    On oft ungrateful soil.
The chalice of your music
    All reverently bear,
For with the blessèd angels
    Such ministry you share.

When you long to bear the Message
    Home to some troubled breast,
Then sing with loving fervour,
    'Come unto Him, and rest.'
Or would you whisper comfort,
    Where words bring no relief,
Sing how 'He was despisèd,
    Acquainted with our grief.'
And, aided by His blessing,
    The song may win its way
Where speech had no admittance,
    And change the night to day.

Sing, when His mighty mercies
    And marvellous love you feel,
And the deep joy of gratitude
    Springs freshly as you kneel;
When words, like morning starlight,
    Melt powerless,—rise and sing!
And bring your sweetest music
    To Him your gracious King.
Pour out your song before Him
    To whom our best is due;
Remember, He who hears your prayer
    Will hear your praises too.

Sing on in grateful gladness!
    Rejoice in this good thing
Which the Lord thy God hath given thee,
    The happy power to sing.
But yield to Him, the Sovereign,
    To whom all gifts belong,
In fullest consecration,
    Your Ministry of Song,
Until His mercy grant you
    That resurrection voice,
Whose only ministry shall be,
    To praise Him and rejoice.

Frances Ridley Havergal

F.R.H.'s manuscript of the single-verse poem "Only for Jesus."

This small card was found among Havergal manuscripts and papers, inexpensive to print and give to many.

Singing for Jesus.

Singing for Jesus, our Saviour & King,
Singing for Jesus, the Lord whom we love!
All adoration we joyously bring,
Longing to praise as they praise Him above.

Singing for Jesus, our Master & Friend,
Telling His love & His marvellous grace,
Love from eternity, love without end,
Love for the loveless, the sinful, & base.

Singing for Jesus, and trying to win
Many to love Him & join in the song;
Calling the weary and wandering in,
Rolling the chorus of gladness along.

Singing for Jesus, our Life & our Light,
Singing for Him as we press to the mark;
Singing for Him when the morning is bright,
Singing, still singing, for Him in the dark!

Singing for Jesus, our Shepherd & Guide,

Singing for gladness of heart that He gives;
Singing for wonder & praise that He died,
Singing for blessing & joy that He lives.

Singing for Jesus, oh singing with joy!
Thus will we praise Him, & tell out His love,
Till He shall call us to brighter employ,
Singing for Jesus for ever above.

June 12.

A poem in F.R.H.'s Manuscript Book Nº VI, written June 12, 1872.

Singing for Jesus.

'With my song will I praise Him.'—PSALM 28:7.

SINGING for Jesus, our Saviour and King,
  Singing for Jesus, the Lord whom we love;
All adoration we joyously bring,
  Longing to praise as we praise Him above.

Singing for Jesus, our Master and Friend,
  Telling His love and His marvellous grace,
Love from eternity, love without end,
  Love for the loveless, the sinful and base.

Singing for Jesus, and trying to win
  Many to love Him, and join in the song;
Calling the weary and wandering in,
  Rolling the chorus of gladness along.

Singing for Jesus, our Life and our Light;
  Singing for Him as we press to the mark;
Singing for Him when the morning is bright,
  Singing, still singing, for Him in the dark.

Singing for Jesus, our Shepherd and Guide,
  Singing for gladness of heart that He gives;
Singing for wonder and praise that He died,
  Singing for blessing and joy that He lives.

Singing for Jesus, oh, singing with joy!
  Thus will we praise Him and tell out His love,
Till He shall call us to brighter employ,
  Singing for Jesus for ever above.

Frances Ridley Havergal

Wayside Chimes — May.

Love for love.

"We have known & believed the love that God hath to us." I John 4.16

Knowing that the God on high,
    With a tender Father's grace,
Waits to hear your faintest cry,
    Waits to show a Father's face, —
Stay & think! oh should not you
Love this gracious Father too?

Knowing Christ was crucified, —
    Knowing that He loves you now
Just as much as when He died
    With the thorns upon His brow, —
Stay & think! oh should not you
Love this blessed Saviour too?

Knowing that a Spirit strives
    With your weary, wandering heart,
Who would change the restless lives,
    Pure & perfect peace impart, —
Stay & think! oh should not you
Love this loving Spirit too?

      Frances Ridley Havergal

This is a fair copy autograph of "Love for Love" in F.R.H.'s hand, which she assigned to a set of poems entitled Wayside Chimes. *This was written late in her life, and the music she wrote for this was one of her last scores.*

STAY AND THINK.

Words and Music by
Frances Ridley Havergal

2. Knowing Christ was crucified,
   Knowing that He loves you now
Just as much as when He died
   With the thorns upon His brow,—
Stay and think! — oh, should not you
Love this blessèd Saviour too?

3. Knowing that a Spirit strives
   With your weary, wandering heart,
Who can change the restless lives,
   Pure and perfect peace impart,—
Stay and think! — oh, should not you
Love this loving Spirit too?

"By Thy Cross and Passion."

" He hath given us rest by His sorrow, and life by His death."—John Bunyan.

WHAT hast Thou done for me, O mighty Friend,
Who lovest to the end!
Reveal Thyself, that I may now behold
Thy love unknown, untold,
Bearing the curse, and made a curse for me,
That blessed and made a blessing I might be.

Oh, Thou wast crowned with thorns, that I might wear
A crown of glory fair;
"Exceeding sorrowful," that I might be
Exceeding glad in Thee;
"Rejected and despised," that I might stand
Accepted and complete on Thy right hand.

Wounded for my transgression, stricken sore,
That I might "sin no more";
Weak, that I might be always strong in Thee;
Bound, that I might be free;
Acquaint with grief, that I might only know
Fulness of joy in everlasting flow.

Thine was the chastisement, with no release,
That mine might be the peace;
The bruising and the cruel stripes were Thine,
That healing might be mine;
Thine was the sentence and the condemnation,
Mine the acquittal and the full salvation.

For Thee revilings, and a mocking throng,
For me the angel-song;
For Thee the frown, the hiding of God's face,
For me His smile of grace;
Sorrows of hell and bitterest death for Thee,
And heaven and everlasting life for me.

Thy cross and passion, and Thy precious death,
While I have mortal breath,
Shall be my spring of love and work and praise,
The life of all my days;
Till all this mystery of love supreme
Be solved in glory—glory's endless theme.

Frances Ridley Havergal

www.ingramcontent.com/pod-product-compliance
Lightning Source LLC
Chambersburg PA
CBHW061725020426
42331CB00006B/1100